Homecoming-Unmasking the Orphan Spirit

Copyright © 2012 Jon P. Voyles, Sr.

All rights reserved. No part of this publication may be reproduced, stored in a retrieval system, or transmitted by any means – electronic, mechanical, photographic (photocopying), recording, or otherwise – without prior permission in writing from the author.

All scriptures used in this book are from the New King James Version, copyright 1983 Thomas Nelson Version.

Take note that the name satan is not capitalized. I choose not to acknowledge him, even to the point of violating grammatical rules.

Printed in the United States of America
ISBN: 13 978-1468137736
ISBN: 10 1468137735

Learn more information at:
www.jesusandasixpack.com

Presented to:

From:

Date:

Table of Contents

FOREWORD	1
INTRODUCTION	3
ORPHAN SPIRIT DEFINED	6
MEET THE ORPHAN	13
WHAT MADE ME AN ORPHAN?	25
THE PRODIGAL	32
IDENTITY CRISIS	38
TRUST	45
VICTIM MENTALITY	53
REVENGE & JUDGMENT	57
PASSIVITY	59
HOPE DEFERRED	62
WHAT ARE YOU SO AFRAID OF?	65
AFFLICTION IS THE MARK OF A SON	74
NOT IN THE BUNK HOUSE	80
SELF RIGHTEOUS	85
WE LOOK TO MAN	91
CONCLUSION	97

ACKNOWLEDGMENTS

I want to thank:

My Abba Father (Daddy God) for all of His insight into writing this book. I can never express my thankfulness to you for choosing me.

My bride Nancy, for your patience and support in all the long hours, late nights and mood swings you endured. I love you for your editing prowess and long hours of reading and re-reading, and re-re-reading!

My family and friends for believing in me.

Shelley Hitz at Self-Publishing-Coach.com, you were definitely a light at the end of a long tunnel with regards to navigating the waters of publishing. Your support, encouragement, and knowledge are appreciated.

Rusty & Tom for believing in me, and seeing the gold God put in me, and putting some of your gold in as well!

Foreword

There are many books and studies in the market place today that explore the topic of being a son or daughter. There are books about understanding the heart of the Father, and if you really want to feel overwhelmed, there is a lot more information on those subjects available through the internet.

How do you digest any or all of that information in a way that allows you to really understand this Father/Child relationship as **the Father** intended? We can barely make our earthly relationships work out within our own families, so how do we really wrap our minds around a heavenly one with a Father that we cannot see, in a realm we do not understand.

My prayer is that this book will help you to identify with some of the attributes and characteristics of an orphan spirit so you can determine if that spirit is in you! If it is, you can never understand being a son of God! Let me say something up front, this is intended for women too, so let's save me the keystrokes of needing to preface everything in this book with daughter and you just know that everything I am writing is for both genders.

This book will hopefully shed some light on what is missing, or better yet, what causes us to miss the mark all too often. The orphan spirit is what causes many believers to never be able to walk in the fullness of the relationship that Jesus died for. It is a spirit that has crippled much of the body of Christ for generations and if this spirit is not dealt with, it will continue to rob you and your family of an amazing breakthrough!

This spirit causes us to walk, talk and live as orphans, yet we are to be a living witness to a lost and dying world about the Good News of the Gospel and, that by the blood of Jesus we are adopted into His family.

Here are some housekeeping issues with regard to this book:

- I refer to satan as ORF throughout the book, Ole Rat Face. That is as affectionate as I want to be with him.
- I use the New King James Version for all of my scriptures (unless stated otherwise) and I have a tendency to put emphasis on particular areas where I am focusing my thought pattern, so if you see something underlined or with **bold font**, emphasis mine.

Introduction

April 28, 2011, at 9:30am, my brother Jim called my cell phone to tell me that my dad had passed away. I knew it was coming. Dad had been sick for years, but you're never really prepared. It was that same morning, just prior to that call, the Lord began to work on me regarding my orphan spirit. I had never even heard of an orphan spirit before but it was manifesting itself in me as a spirit of rebellion, especially in regards to my work.

It is amazing how intertwined that deceptive spirit gets in our lives and in our hearts. It affects every area of our life and we cannot ignore it. In the course of reading this book, there will probably be areas of your own life where you see this manifested. If you do not address it when it is revealed and deal with it, just like every other sin, it will continue to grow and it will be just that much harder to gain complete victory over it.

Much of my revelation came from Luke 15, the story about the prodigal son. What surprised me in this study was not the attitude and actions of the prodigal, but of his brother. I realized that this brother was dealing with more deep seated issues in the spiritual realm than the brother who squandered his father's money on an obviously sinful lifestyle. I felt the Lord show me that I could relate more to the older brother in my current walk as a believer than the prodigal.

We are sometimes swept away by this amazing story of a loving, forgiving and extravagant Father. The Lord revealed to me that there is another purpose inside this parable as well, intended to warn us about what we are doing in the church as a body of believers even today! The story of the prodigal tells of the bondages of <u>both</u> brothers. When you read the story, you will see the older brother that stayed was living, breathing and acting as an orphan...yet he was a son. He had the religious piety and works mentality down to a science, as he defended his actions as to why he would not attend his brother's party. He had all the verbiage and attitudes of an orphan.

In my research and discussions regarding the orphan spirit, I have come across a few "older brother" believers that have been rather, shall we say, guarded and less than open minded regarding the orphan spirit. I am well aware that as I even mention the orphan spirit, I know some of you who are reading this may question me as to where it actually says orphan spirit in the Bible. I will let you in on a secret, it doesn't say those exact words; however, the Bible isn't a black and white text book. It is a **living word** and it gives us insight, wisdom and knowledge of the spirit realm and warns us that our warfare is in *that* realm.

The heart will never accept the truth if it believes a lie.

I have literally had dozens of people come to me and tell me how after they heard me speak on this subject that God opened their eyes and hearts to this spirit. They were shocked and amazed how they were actively operating in this spirit and never even realized it.

While there is no way to provide a comprehensive list of all the ways that the orphan spirit may manifest, we will discuss many different lies, or fruits from the orphan tree, that cause us to believe those lies. Some of these are:

- Affliction
- Rejection
- Fear
- Vengeance
- Passivity
- Acceptance
- Strife & Competition

When you read this book, do it with an open heart and mind and do not allow preconceived thoughts, religion, denomination or doctrine beliefs to get in the way.

Read this book, pray for the Father to let you see His heart, and let's kill a fatted calf together at the end. We will make merry, be glad, and have a party...with our brothers! By the way, I like my fatted calf medium rare! ☺

Chapter 1

Orphan spirit defined

What is the definition of an orphan?

- A child who has been deprived of parental care and has not been adopted
- One that lacks support, supervision, or care

There are more definitions, but this is what I feel is necessary to get to the root of what is being discussed in this book, so let's only use the definitions that apply to the topic being addressed.

My understanding is that an orphan is someone who is not, or is no longer a son or daughter because of some circumstance, and is not being provided for by a parental influence. Another way to look at it is, if you are not a son, then what are you? If you are not <u>His</u> kid, what are you? **An orphan!**

Let me clarify something. We are not talking about salvation. That is an entirely different subject. We are dealing with a mindset, attitude and bondage that will keep a son from living <u>freely</u> in the fullness and benefit of the Father's blessings. A spirit that we freely pick up and lay down in our lives that will always cause us to see the Father in a way that is not accurate or better yet, that is a lie!

The very basis and foundation of this book is to understand that *we do not wrestle against flesh and blood, but against principalities, against powers, against the rulers of the darkness of this age, against spiritual hosts of wickedness in the heavenly places, as Ephesians 6:12* tells us.

This passage of scripture helped me press through my doubts and fears with regards to writing about this topic. I realized that even though the words "orphan spirit" were not written specifically in black and white in the Bible, it didn't mean that it wasn't there, and it doesn't mean that we don't struggle with it.

I know that I know that God told me to write and teach about this. Combining that knowledge with the resistance that I have met regarding this subject is evidence enough for me to see that it is there. Once my eyes were opened to this spirit, I saw it being manifested in His sons and they were oblivious to their own words, actions, rebellion, and mannerisms that were screaming out "orphan".

Please hear my heart regarding this, I am writing this to **help** my family in Christ. To clarify what I mean; some make it all about what they are doing or about what religious act has to be performed in order to please God…HE IS ALREADY PLEASED! God sees us through the blood of Jesus and that is more than enough to set us free from our past, present and future unrighteousness!

What about your yesterday are you listening to today that affects your tomorrow?

Is it that you have failed? Is it about your sin? Or is it about your victories? If it is sin and failure, you are missing the greatest gift of all! Freedom!

Since God sees His kids through the blood of Jesus…He doesn't see your sin! He sees His child, a child who is in a spiritual battle, and His desire is for them to finish well. If we can lay our heads on our pillows at night knowing that He is pleased with us then we can get up tomorrow with a positive attitude to wage war and fight the good fight!

We can have a more victorious tomorrow if we stop going to bed defeated today!

I pray God's mercy and grace on that person that only sees the failure, and I pray God's peace and understanding on the church that only preaches Hellfire and Brimstone. The Word talks about His love for us WAY more than it does anything else.

Ask yourself these questions:

- Do you see the Father as an angry tyrant just looking for a reason to take you down?
- Do you see Him as someone that has no tolerance for any mistake?
- Do you have a perverted sense of duty rather than relationship with the Father? (you are all about what YOU have to do or are doing FOR HIM, rather than sharing with others what HE has done for YOU)

If your answer was yes to any (or all) of the questions above, then you may be struggling with an orphan spirit. Even if you don't see the orphan spirit, you will still see Him with a filtered view that He never intended. Romans 2 tells us that *it is the goodness of God that leads man to repentance*….not the penance, or the Holy Ghost smack down!

Paul shares with us in Romans 6:1 that when we realize we have been given this grace and mercy from the Father, we won't want to sin more; we will desire to sin less, BECAUSE of that freedom!

HE LOVES YOU and wants you to walk in freedom, love and acceptance.

Luke 4:18 ^{18} *"The Spirit of the LORD is upon Me, because He has anointed Me, to preach the gospel to the poor; He has sent Me to heal the brokenhearted, to proclaim liberty to the captives and recovery of sight to the blind, to set at liberty those who are oppressed;*

His desire is <u>for you</u> and for your freedom. For you to walk free from the bondages and spiritual funk of this world! That is the Good News, which is the great commission to lead others in the truth!

If all we show the world a bunch of rules, regulations, religious duties, or denominational practices (**demon**inational as I like to call it), then all we are doing is leading them from bondage to bondage, or from their bondage to yours.

I need to clarify something from that last comment; I have nothing against denominations, unless that is where you get your identity or it causes division. It is an organization not a religion. When people ask what you believe in are you telling them Presbyterian or Christian? You should be relating to the God over that church, not the church.

I am writing this book to set the captives free. As a matter of fact, throughout the writing of this book, those are the words that keep resounding in my spirit...set the captives free. I have had several people pray over me and speak those words or words very similar to them about this book as well. I am not writing this for fame, fortune or notoriety. I am writing this because the Lord spoke to me on at least a half dozen occasions and specifically pointed out this spirit in my life, and then told me to share that with others. It is out of my own relationship with Jesus that I desire to write this, not out of duty.

Our lives of freedom from bondage show the Great Commission much louder than trying to teach it when we don't live it.

All I am asking the reader to do is continue on the pages of this book and allow the Holy Spirit to speak to you about your own heart, and to see if there is anything that the Lord wants to reveal to you, personally.

God's desire is **for you,** and for you to be liberated from the captivity of wrong thinking and wrong doctrine. His desire is for you to understand His Word as a love letter, and a living Word. The Bible was never intended to be a text book or encyclopedia of doctrine. It is a love story that adapts to the different situations and stages of life. It guides us in truth and knowledge of His desire for us.

When we misunderstand the intent of the Father's heart we miss it. Interestingly, sin is actually an archery term that means to miss the mark. It isn't that we intentionally go out to willfully sin, sometimes we just miss it. It grieves the Father to see his children in bondage to sin, or to themselves. That is why he sent Jesus.

The following scripture is an example of an orphan spirit that is actively working in the heart of a son. He is in the father's house but doesn't live like a son.

Luke 15:28-32 (NKJV) [28] *"But he was angry and would not go in. Therefore his father came out and pleaded with him.* [29] *So he answered and said to his father, 'Lo, these many years I have been serving you; I never transgressed your commandment at any time; and yet you never gave me a young goat that I might make merry with my friends.* [30] *But as soon as this son of yours came, who has devoured your livelihood with harlots, you killed the fatted calf for him.'* [31] *"And he said to him, 'Son, you are always with me, and all that I have is yours.* [32] *It was right that we should make merry and be glad, for your brother was dead and is alive again, and was lost and is found.'"*

He is not focused at all on the restoration of his lost brother. He is not rejoiced that his own flesh and blood is not dead! He is only focused on what he perceives that he is not getting! Yet the father tells him that ALL the father has is his. He is in the father's house for years and all he is concerned with is being in the fields doing the work, what he is doing for the father? Where is the relationship? Where is the intimacy?

Those questions will cause an orphan to get really uncomfortable! *Hosea 4:6 says that My people will be destroyed for lack of knowledge*! The word used for knowledge is Da'ath but the root of that word is Yada, the same intimate act as when Adam "knew" Eve...that's intimate! There is more on this subject later on in the book.

Another point that needs to be addressed is, when have you ever had a conversation with your Dad about your brother and spoke it like this; "As soon as <u>this son</u> of yours came, who had devoured <u>your</u> livelihood..."? Really? You would have said "Dad, I can't believe you let Jim get away with this". My point is that from his own mouth, he was speaking as an orphan, with the intent to <u>separate himself from the father</u>, and his brother. He is speaking and acting like an orphan in the father's house.

Luke 6:45 tells us that *out of the abundance of the heart, the mouth speak.* Sounds to me like his heart is not one of a son, but of an orphan.

In the next chapter we will meet a fictional character that portrays the heart of an orphan. He said the prayer, got his "fire insurance", but his heart never received the adoption papers. He never really got what the Lord wanted him to have. If all we ever got from the Cross was a back stage pass to heaven, what a waste!

Jesus died for our relationship with the Father to be restored.

The story may be fictional but I believe it depicts the average Christian today, the struggles that you face especially with regards to never entering into the Father's house, taking off your shoes and plopping down on the couch <u>with Him</u>.

It is about relationship!

Chapter 2

Meet the orphan

He is an average American with a family, bills, a job, and maybe even a relationship with "his" God. But let's look deeper at his life...

He could be short tempered, may strive for attention, and probably is very competitive, looking to the world for what should and can only be provided to him by God. He struggles in his marriage, struggles with sexual sin, rejection, acceptance, alcoholism and struggles in relationships. He definitely struggles with trust and faith. Each one of his struggles usually causes conflict with other struggles because they are related, yet he doesn't see it. He is oblivious to it. As a matter of fact, he will usually blame outside influences for it, and everything else is at fault. He just can't seem to "get a break". He will blame his wife, kids, boss, client, church, friends...or lack thereof, but all of it stems from something that he doesn't even recognize that he lives out, and he lives it out loud! He says and does things that separate him from God (he orphans himself) and yet doesn't understand how or why God would do this **to** him. He battles with an orphan spirit. Now that may not come as a surprise to some of you, but you may be surprised to find out that many of you are struggling just like him! Let's meet him.

<u>A day in the life of an orphan, Scott:</u>

Scott is married to Rebecca and they have 2 teenage kids. They are your average American family that has grown accustomed to a certain upper middle class lifestyle, much like the ones they grew up in. They have a decent marriage, don't fight... much, but there are some topics and issues that they choose not to discuss or avoid at all costs. They are a rather normal couple.

Neither Scott nor Rebecca is much for the church but they attend somewhat regularly. They grew up going but never got involved outside the normal attendance and maybe a summer retreat if they knew their friends were going. They prefer to think that since they are good people they will be accepted into heaven, and after all, they said the prayer of salvation back in Sunday school. They prefer the cafeteria approach to God and church. They take whatever fits and what they like and compile that into their own personal belief system, and they function quite nicely, thank you very much!

Scott is a local businessman in copier sales. His work is centered on meeting new people, cultivating relationships and providing service after the sale. It is a tough job since every day he wakes up he feels unemployed. Unless he goes out and makes it happen, it doesn't. No one seems to understand that the pressure is *all on him* to get it done.

 Scott has had a certain level of success but seems to struggle with truly breaking out of his own self-imposed mold, if you will, of mediocrity. He doesn't really understand how God could be blessing him if there are so many darn speed bumps and struggles in this world. He may or may not go to church; the church may be his problem. After all, isn't that just a religious, greedy, social club? But nonetheless, to appease his conscience and his wife, he has become just a little more consistent than a CEO Christian. (Said the prayer and goes to church on Christmas/Easter Only)

He works in a competitive market with a lot of challenges, but Scott is quite confident in his knowledge and abilities. Scott has a love/hate relationship with his job since he has a tendency to get acceptance and identity from his career and financial status. But it also causes him and all those around him to suffer from the roller coaster ride when things don't go his way.

One of Scott's many problems is his temper and his untamed tongue. It has cost him many a friendship, a few sales/clients, and has even caused his dad to speak only to him on holidays. Scott says that his temper is nothing more than a reflection of his dad growing up. His dad was a hot head; I guess he got that too. His parents loved him and cared for him and provided a decent upper middle class lifestyle, so he can't complain...but yet somehow, he still does!

Scott likes to unwind after a hard day and relax with his wife and knock back a few. He isn't hurting anyone. He doesn't drink and drive...much, although there is the issue of that DUI he got a few years back. He is much more careful now...and knows the back roads home if for some reason he does slip up.

Scott and Rebecca's kids are your typical teens that have the same relationship with God that their parents do, and if they stay below the radar, they can get away with quite a bit.

Behind the closed doors of their house are some dangerous undercurrents that they all know are there, but they seem to live quite out of touch with reality concerning any way of dealing with them. They argue over seemingly silly issues to an outsider, and have even lost their tempers over those issue and fallen into the cycle of silent treatments and making up, or possibly not making up but just sweeping it under the rug and acting like it never happened (boy is that rug getting dirty!). Sadly, there are issues, and there are times when they go to bed angry, or someone gets to sleep on the couch. The silent treatment is a normal occurrence; the only variation is how long it lasts.

But, here is where the problems get deeper for Scott and Rebecca; they don't stand a chance of winning the battle in these areas if they have no clue where the fight is coming from.

Scott gets ready to leave for the day; kids are off to school...

Rebecca says, "So are you going to close that deal any time soon with the Medical Clinic?"

Scott, "I'm sure gonna try. Geez it has been 4 months of that guy yanking my chain... just buy the stupid thing old man."

Rebecca, "What's taking him so long?"

Scott, "Not sure. I have run countless difference price quotes and service agreements past him; we have the best price and service so I am sure we will get it. Just need to convince **him** of that."

Rebecca, "Do you think he is shopping around?"

Scott, "I don't think so, at least he hasn't brought anyone up in our conversations."

Rebecca, "Well I wish you would just get this sold so we can take the kids to Florida like we keep promising them we will."

Scott, "Wow, no pressure there!"

Rebecca, "You know what I mean! You promised the kids we would go and your job is the only one that provides the opportunity for us to do things like that. I don't get a chance for bonuses as a book keeper at a hotel!"

Scott, "I know, I know, but I got enough pressure from the Regional Sales guy right now and I don't need more from you!"

Rebecca, "Sorry!"

Scott, "That fine, whatever."

Rebecca, "My sister said she is praying for us, so I'll say a little prayer for you today. What time is your appointment?"

Scott, "1:30 this afternoon. Tell your Holy Roller sis 'the church lady' to pray hard. I've worked my butt off on this sale and I deserve to get it!"

Rebecca, "Ok will do, love you."

Scott, "Love you too."

Scott leaves for the day….

It is 1:12pm in the parking lot of the Family Medical Center.

Scott sits in his car looking over the proposal once again to be sure he has all his ducks in a row before he goes in. "I've gotta make this sale" he says. His thoughts are on the proposal but his mind wanders to Rebecca's comment about her sister Debbie, "praying for us" he says...well I guess it never hurts so he says his own prayer in the car. "God, I am asking for your favor on this deal. You know how hard I have worked and all the countless hours I have put into this. All I am asking is for you to get Tom to make the decision in my favor. I want to take my wife and kids on that vacation. Please provide like the pastor said in his sermon last month, you were the provider, Jehovah something or other, so please provide. Oh, and thanks God. Amen."

He looks over the proposals one last time and heads in to meet with the director, Tom.

"He's ready for you," says his secretary.

"Thank you," Scott says with a big smile. He was definitely noticing her where he was waiting for the last 30 minutes. "She's hot", he thinks as he walks into Tom's office.

"Hello Scott. Come on in and have a seat," says Tom.

"How are things?" responds Scott

"Good Scott, thank you for asking. Don't mean to be short with you but I have a full schedule today so let's get right down to this," says Tom.

"Great, I am ready to get this taken care of too", he says while thinking to himself "let's get down to you approving this sale!"

"It's been a bit of a journey for us to get this handled, huh" jokes Scott while thinking to himself, "you are the one that keeps putting this off, write the check old man!" He laughs to himself as he opens up his briefcase, and pulls out the proposal.

As they look over the numbers of the proposal, Tom sits back in his chair and says, "Scott, is this your rock bottom for this deal?"

"I'm losing money as it is, but I will make it up in volume", he jokes.

"I appreciate all the hard work and diligence that you have shown me, but I have to tell you that I have been talking with a guy at Minolta and they have provided us with a better price and service package."

Scott is shocked and stunned at this. "He never told me I was in competition with Minolta," he thinks.

"Scott, I have already made my decision to go with Minolta. I appreciate your work and would like to stay in touch with you for the future though," says Tom.

Scott doesn't know what to say...he feels the blood rush to his face, he feels that old familiar feeling of rejection and the anger that follows it and as he processes the feeling, before he even realizes it, he is speaking...loudly.

"This is a total rip, you have been jerking me around for 4 months, wasting my time and efforts just so you can stab me in the back. Well thanks for nothing!" he shouts.

Before Tom could respond from his obvious astonishment about Scott's outburst, Scott is already throwing things into his briefcase and he storms out the door.

As Scott slams the door on his car and tears out the parking lot, spinning tires, he sarcastically says to God "fat lot of good it did praying to you! Where were you? Why didn't you help? Apparently you don't care about me! You must love your precious Minolta copier guy more!"

5:40pm

Scott pulls into his driveway and he doesn't want to go inside. He anticipates what the response will be when he has to tell Rebecca what happened. He contemplates coming up with a lie, but since he has been at the bar most of the afternoon, he can't come up with anything good.

"So, how'd it go?" Rebecca asks cheerfully.

"Apparently praying doesn't work!" barks Scott, as he tosses his briefcase on the dining room chair.

"What? Did you not get it?" asks Rebecca.

"No, I didn't! So we can kiss the Florida trip goodbye. Apparently God wants the Minolta guy to take his family instead!" says Scott.

"I'm sorry Hun..." says Rebecca as she comes to give him a hug.

Then a pause

"Have you been drinking?" she asks

"Ya, it just got me so angry I didn't know what to do." confesses Scott.

"And you drove? Scott, we can hardly afford to pay our insurance premiums from your DUI 2 years ago. What were you thinking?" asks Rebecca.

"Great, lets add a little guilt trip about the past to an already horrible day, and I didn't get pulled over. I am not drunk!" yells Scott.

"Whatever," says Rebecca as she storms off.

"Whatever is right!" Scott yells as he heads to the garage.

Scott and Rebecca don't talk to each other through dinner and the kids are well aware of the tension, so they hurry through dinner and head off to their rooms.

10:03pm

Rebecca went to bed at 9:00 and Scott stayed up and watched some TV. As he is watching the sports highlights he sees an ad for Minolta. That stirs up that pain in stomach once again. He sits on the couch and runs the scenario over in his head for the hundredth time since he stormed out of Tom's office. Regret over his reaction to Tom is gnawing at him. As he is thinking, he can't help but be angry. "Where was God in all of this?" he asks to himself.

Then his mind goes to Rebecca and the kids, the trip, etc. As he is on the couch, finishing off his last drink of the night he replays the scenario for one last time and he remembers something from that day...the secretary. She was cute. As he thinks about her, he is reminded that she looks a lot like the actress from that TV show. "Maybe I will just go look up a picture of that actress from the show," he thinks.

11:30pm

Scott is sitting nervously at this computer keeping his ear as keenly tuned as he can, making sure Rebecca doesn't come out of the bedroom. What started as a simple temptation to look on the internet for a picture of an actress has Scott now surfing porn on the family computer. As he is scanning the images, he is going further and further than he ever anticipated....

"What is that!" yells Rebecca.

Scott didn't realize that between the dulling of his senses from the drinks and the distraction of what he was looking at, she had caught him.

"How long have you been doing this?" she asks angrily with her arms folded across her chest.

"I, I just... just got caught up in it," Scott pleads.

"Can this day get any worse?" thinks Scott as Rebecca storms off to the bedroom and he hears a resounding click of the door locking after she slams it shut.

To take us from this totally fictional story of what can happen in everyday life, we see many things in Scott and Rebecca's life where, without any knowledge whatsoever, they are in an full on battle with the orphan spirit.

Sound familiar to you? Have you ever lost your temper with God? You may not have said these things out loud to God, but you said them in your heart and your actions, and that is no different in God's eyes. Scott's problem is an orphan spirit, and even though he may have read a book about sonship and the heart of the Father, he doesn't get it! He CAN'T get it! He is cloaked with an orphan spirit and he will never understand unless the Father reveals this to him!

The issue goes deeper, much deeper into the very psyche of his relationships with everyone and everything! You can be orphaned in an infinite amount of ways:

- Old girlfriend/boyfriend
- Church
- Jobs
- Or even lost sales opportunities

It can grab a hold of anyone; we are ALL susceptible to adopting an orphan spirit. No one is immune.

We have all acted like an orphan at some time. Some of the more common manifestations are:

- Worrying
- Striving or Competition
- Fighting
- Kicking against the goads
- Shrinking back
- Rebelling
- Acting out
- Offering ourselves to idols...booze, bikes, broads
- Denying Him

There is an endless list of things that we can do that don't line up with someone who is a true son of God.

Did Jesus ever do this? He was adopted! Joseph adopted Jesus as his son and so if we look at that scenario, Jesus himself should have struggled with the same issues as the Scott in our story. What is the difference? Why did Jesus react in the manner that He did when He was faced with extreme rejection?

He knew He was a Son, not an orphan.

Chapter 3

What made <u>me</u> an orphan?

Our Father will never orphan us, so who does? Or what does? Can circumstances or situations? Yes. I was orphaned; not by my parents and not by God (obviously), but my orphan spirit was tied to the church. Here is part of my story…

I was saved in a Baptist Church in central Missouri as a kid, about 13. I know that day that I gave my life, when I said that prayer, I meant it (as fire insurance) but I meant it nonetheless. Fast forward to age 17. I had moved to Colorado when my dad took a job transfer, and during that time I was working at The Original Hamburger Stand. There was a girl working there that I really liked, and I asked her to go out on a date. She said the only way she could was if her dad said yes. He was a Minister of the Baptist Church in that town so since I had been to the Baptist church and got saved in the Baptist church, I thought this is a "shoo-in". I was certain that he would like me because of my background in the church. I would simply add some charm coupled with relating to him from my Baptist roots. You know the routine.

Well, was I in for a surprise! He was not a nice person. You may be saying that he looked at me as a wolf in sheep's clothing, but truthfully he never even got to know me well enough to make that judgment. He was just rude and mean to me. As a matter of fact, I can honestly say that I never once saw the love of Christ in him. So I confronted him and asked "what is your problem with me. I have never done anything to you." His response, "when I see a guy with long hair and an earring, I want to give him one of these." as he held his fist up to my face. Nice, huh! Feeling the love of Jesus there! My hair was to my collar and I had 1 small stud earring (what can I say, it was the 80's). That comment started a 15 year Saul journey for me. Yes, that comment pissed me off, and ORF (Ole Rat Face satan) used it to bring me an orphan spirit. In my anger I took on that spirit with zeal. I swear that I met every fruit, nut and flake in the Christian bowl after that experience. It was what pushed me farther and farther from the Father! And I grew my hair to the middle of my back and had 4 earrings...do you see some rebelling by an orphan here? I do now! And here I am, 28 years after that lovely experience, realizing that I am still struggling with that same stupid spirit!

Be careful what you say to others! Hold your tongue as James said! You have no idea what your words can do!

I can honestly say that I no longer hold the un-forgiveness in my heart towards that pastor. He could have repented an hour later. I was the prisoner of my own anger, and that orphan spirit I picked up for all those years.

My point is simple; you can be orphaned from the family of God, from God, from His plan, etc. Really it is anything that keeps you from Him. Anything that separates your communication with Him. Anything that distracts, perverts, or wages war against Him. We battle not against flesh and blood, but against principalities, powers, and rulers of darkness...or do we?

We don't always war in the way that the Bible tells us. Actually we war exactly wrong all too often; by worrying, doubting and complaining. But as children of God, we have the confidence that we hear from Him as it says in, *John 10:27* **27** *My sheep hear My voice, and I know them, and they follow Me.*

We also have the confidence that we are NOT orphans. *John 10:28-29 neither shall anyone snatch them out of My hand, My Father has given them to Me.*

John 15:16-17 You did NOT choose Me, but I chose you and appointed you that you should go and bear fruit and that your fruit should remain, that whatever you ask the Father in My name He may give you! I command you, love one another.

That is one way we can orphan others, by not loving them. I am walking proof of that! What we miss is that Jesus told us to love one another; it is equal to loving the Lord with all your heart, mind, soul, and strength! What is missing in the church sometimes is not programs or outreaches, its love! We need to be leading others to His love!

There is no defense against love. Think about it. The world has an answer for judgment, answer for condemnation, guilt, fear, fire and brimstone...but what is the defense against love? Love conquers all! Do you have the ability to keep hating someone that loves you? In the way that Jesus did? Do you have a counter attack for love? I know I didn't.

Back to my testimony, now I am 30 years old, long hair, a jerk, drink too much, not a nice guy. Hurting and making everyone else around me hurt too so I don't feel orphaned.

An orphan will make orphans of others so they don't feel all alone.

I get invited to a men's ministry event by my drinking buddy. He had just accepted Christ and had his own orphan spirit issues. Anyways, he invited me to this saying that it was just a bunch of guys that got together and discussed their challenges. He lied!

He didn't tell me that it was a full blown active body of Christ men's ministry that was evangelizing and reaching out to hurting and lost souls, and here is the kicker; they had the nerve to love me. I was not ready for it, trust me.

So I pulled into the parking lot, and said to God, "I am going to get even with You for all the years of hurt You brought me! Bring the biggest guy You got, because the first guy that says anything about my hair I am going to drill in the mouth." (my defense was offense). I had accepted the orphan lie that all Christians hated long hair and judged me based on my appearance and would never look at the person I could be. That you were nothing more than your appearance and unless you act like them you can't get into heaven. Trust me; there are some Christians that act this harshly towards the lost. Why would they want to spend eternity with a bunch of judgmental jackasses? (Sorry, but it is true)

Quick question, what about you draws the lost TO you? Is it your "loftiness" that you are not as lost as them? Is it your judgment of them? Or is it because of your unconditional love FOR them...like Jesus? Remember Dudley Do Right that Jesus hung with tax collectors and sinners, called them friends!

John 11:19 ⁱ⁹ The Son of Man came eating and drinking, and they say, 'Look, a glutton and a winebibber, a friend of tax collectors and sinners!'

Take that scripture and put it in your heart (as well as your pipe and smoke it). The very same Jesus you claim to serve was not judging those around Him but loving them **into** the Kingdom...are you?

I digress....when I walked into the church; I was fully ready for a fist fight (and a trip to jail). I kid you not. I wanted to hurt someone as much as I was hurting. After all, I believed that it was the church that orphaned me (actually it was man, but he represented the church). I walked in fully expecting what I had experienced before (by the way, most people do) and what I got hit with I had no defense for. A little old silver haired man walks up to me, (I am thinking I don't want to drill the old dude, but I will) and to my shock and disbelief, he put his arms around me (not a side hug like most guys do) but a "putting it all out there" hug and with his head on my chest said, "I love you, and it is great to have you here." I cannot express the thanks that I have to that man even as I write this.

Some nerve this guy had, to love on me when I didn't even ask for it. My problem now is that I have no idea who it is or was. I don't even know if it was an angel or a man. It couldn't have been easy; I walked in with hate in my heart, alcohol on my breath and was completely sidelined by love.

A total leg sweep of love that took me down.

I didn't know what to say, or do for that matter. And to make matters worse, when I looked around and saw bikers hugging guys in suits, my thought was "what the hell is this". I had not experienced this unabashed, unrestricted love of Jesus before, so this was ALL new to me.

Great! Just great. I have no reason to leave now (I hadn't planned on actually staying). Now I had to stay and listen to the message. I could not tell you what the message was about. It didn't matter though, because I got the message at the door with a hug. God loves me! I gave my life to the Lord the next day, I had to. I couldn't resist what had happened to me. All of my secular doctrine of what the church represented and what God was in my mind, was all wrong. Someone blew up my island and I had nowhere to stand, so I had to begin looking for dry land. It was that single random act of unabashed love that rocked me to the core and caused me to look deeper. Not just at myself but if all that I had thought was and was not God. What do I do? Where do I go from here?

If you have not experienced that kind of love or that you have experienced something similar to my experience, let me be the first to say from the body of Christ, I am sorry!

Jesus died for you too and since you are good enough for Him, you are good enough for all of us. I am writing this book to YOU, because I want you to experience the Love of Jesus, the Love of the Father, the reason Jesus came….you! You are really that special to the Father! He desires relationship and communication with you! Why don't you talk to Him right now, not like He isn't there because **He is with you** right where you are, He is in the room….talk to Him…He cares!

If you are not a believer but now feel that "tug" in your heart let me offer you some hope, some dry land.

Romans 10:9-10 "if you confess with your mouth the Lord Jesus and believe in your heart that God has raised Him from the dead, you will be saved. For with the heart one believes to righteousness, and with the mouth confession is made to salvation".

That "tug" you feel is your heart believing in Him. Let's take it to the next level...confess with your mouth.

Say this prayer:

Lord, I now know that I am a sinner and that if I believe in You that I will be saved. I want to be saved. I want to know you. I want to be your son/daughter. Please forgive me of all my sins and help me to see You as You truly are. Wash me white as snow in the blood of Jesus. Jesus come into my heart. I want You to be my personal Lord and Savior.

Welcome to the family! Your salvation is a free gift and His desire is for you to receive it and especially, walk in it. Take the time to read His Word, not as a "work" but as someone who desires to know Him more.

Chapter 4

The Prodigal

The basis of this book was derived from a revelation of this scripture; read it a couple of times if necessary.

Luk 15:11-32 And he said, A certain man had two sons:
And the younger of them said to his father, Father, give me the portion of goods that falleth to me. And he divided unto them his living.
And not many days after the younger son gathered all together, and took his journey into a far country, and there wasted his substance with riotous living.
And when he had spent all, there arose a mighty famine in that land; and he began to be in want.
And he went and joined himself to a citizen of that country; and he sent him into his fields to feed swine.
And he would fain have filled his belly with the husks that the swine did eat: and no man gave unto him.
And when he came to himself, he said, How many hired servants of my father's have bread enough and to spare, and I perish with hunger!
I will arise and go to my father, and will say unto him, Father, I have sinned against heaven, and before thee,
And am no more worthy to be called thy son: make me as one of thy hired servants.
And he arose, and came to his father. But when he was yet a great way off, his father saw him, and had compassion, and ran, and fell on his neck, and kissed him.
And the son said unto him, Father, I have sinned against heaven, and in thy sight, and am no more worthy to be called thy son.

> But the father said to his servants, Bring forth the best robe, and put it on him; and put a ring on his hand, and shoes on his feet:
> And bring hither the fatted calf, and kill it; and let us eat, and be merry:
> For this my son was dead, and is alive again; he was lost, and is found. And they began to be merry.
> Now his elder son was in the field: and as he came and drew nigh to the house, he heard music and dancing.
> And he called one of the servants, and asked what these things meant.
> And he said unto him, Thy brother is come; and thy father hath killed the fatted calf, because he hath received him safe and sound.
> And he was angry, and would not go in: therefore came his father out, and intreated him.
> And he answering said to his father, Lo, these many years do I serve thee, neither transgressed I at any time thy commandment: and yet thou never gavest me a kid, that I might make merry with my friends:
> But as soon as this thy son was come, which hath devoured thy living with harlots, thou hast killed for him the fatted calf.
> And he said unto him, Son, thou art ever with me, and all that I have is thine.
> It was meet that we should make merry, and be glad: for this thy brother was dead, and is alive again; and was lost, and is found.

Let's start with the brother who left, let's face it. We have all sinned and fallen short of the glory of God. That is scriptural. We have all, at one point or another in our lives, been able to relate to this brother. We also can relate to the mental gymnastics that he played with coming back to the Father.

He played out in his head how it would go, not truly knowing the actual outcome. *I will arise and go to my father, and will say unto him, Father; I have sinned against heaven, and before thee, and am no more worthy to be called thy son: make me as one of thy hired servants.*

How many times have you been in sin, and in your repentance played out in your head how it would look when you return to Him? What the conditions would be for acceptance? What His response would be?

Has it ever worked out exactly as you have thought? Not for me. As a matter of fact, thankfully I have lived Romans 2:4 far too often. *Or do you despise the riches of His goodness, forbearance and longsuffering, not knowing that it is* **the goodness of God that leads man to repentance***?*

It is His goodness that bought me, got me, and brought me to Him. His goodness is the only thing that will still work today. When we are struggling with an orphan spirit, we cannot accept the love of a Father. We think that He cannot love us because of….you fill in the blank. We cannot run to Him when we are afraid of Him (not to be confused with the fear of the Lord). We will always try to play it out in our heads, and that is a battle ground that some of us have no weapons to work with. ☺

Eph 6:12 We wrestle NOT against flesh and blood but against principalities, powers and rulers of darkness of this age, and against spiritual hosts of wickedness in heavenly places. We are battling a spiritual battle with a fleshly mind. Talk about bringing a butter knife to a gun fight!

We need to let go of our knowledge to attain His.

We need to embrace the heart of the Father, to know Him as it says in His Word, in order to truly grasp His love for us. It can and will radically change us from the inside out.

It changes the ball game entirely when we realize that it is His heart to simply be close to us, without all the religion, doctrine, and games that seem to interrupt the intimacy He so desperately desires, and we so desperately need!

Going back to the prodigal son, we see that the father didn't give a rip about having another employee, he wanted a son! He saw a son, not a servant! To live to the fullness of a son we have to see ourselves as a son. We have to stop acting like we think we know what God wants; this prodigal is a great example!

HOWEVER:

If we look at the story again we see something very unique. In all my 15 years of attending church, listening to pastors and reading books, I have never heard anyone address the other brother. Both brothers in the parable of the prodigal had an orphan spirit. Not only did the prodigal have it, but this brother walked in it in a much stronger way, and he was totally clueless to it.

When we look at the older brother's response to the salvation/restoration of his own flesh and blood, we see something interesting.

Luke 15:25-32 Now his elder son was in the field: and as he came and drew nigh to the house, he heard music and dancing. And he called one of the servants, and asked what these things meant. And he said unto him, Thy brother is come; and thy father hath killed the fatted calf, because he hath received him safe and sound. And he was angry, and would not go in: therefore came his father out, and intreated him. And he answering said to his father, Lo, these many years do I serve thee, neither transgressed I at any time thy commandment: and yet thou never gavest me a kid, that I might make merry with my friends: But as soon as this thy son was come, which hath devoured thy living with harlots, thou hast killed for him the fatted calf. And he said unto him, Son, thou art ever with me, and all that I have is thine. It was meet that we should make merry, and be glad: for this thy brother was dead, and is alive again; and was lost, and is found.

This rocked my world when the Lord revealed it to me. This older brother acted much more like an orphan than the prodigal. Let me paint the picture: here you are, a son of the father (an extravagantly loving father by the way) that obviously cared deeply for his children, (after all, didn't he go out to meet both)? You are in His house every day but yet all you desire to do is the work? Your identity and relationship with Him is tied to your work in the field? What you do "for" Him? Keeping His commandments? Not transgressing? Forsaking the actual partaking of a goat or calf as a sense of righteousness?

Sounds to me like an orphan that is trying to achieve "employee of the month", rather than a son that is in right relationship with the father, realizing that the father would hold NOTHING back from him. That ALL the father has is his to take. Not just his portion but ALL! If this brother would stop competing for his father's attention and just embrace it, he would have it all.

Does this sound at all like the church today? And please note I am part of the church and I am not picking on the church. I was blown away because I realized that I do this myself. I can be so easily offended when I see the Father extravagantly show His love to my brother or sister, not knowing that ALL He has is for me to partake in as well! Here I am living in the house of the Almighty God, living with the mentality of an orphan.

It is a law of recognition; if I just looked around, I would recognize that all I need is right before me. All I need is already there, and I just need to "in faith" reach out and take it. Trust me on this, if the body of Christ starts to live and breathe like we are **already** living in the Father's house... Ole Rat Face is in big trouble!

There is also a practical application of this knowledge too. We need to have more than just **knowledge of** the Father's heart towards us. Here is my thought. You can read about the Father's love and read about being a son, but have you experienced it? I have watched someone race a car at 200 MPH around a track, but until I have actually done it, I cannot say that I have fully experienced it. It is the practical application of that knowledge, because knowing it just isn't enough! The Father's heart is for you to fully **experience** His love, not just know *about* it. An orphan cannot "know" it, and that is why ORF wants to keep you from that experiential knowledge. After all, he **is,** and will always be, an orphan.

Chapter 5

Identity Crisis

Identity theft started in the Garden of Eden. The body of Christ is targeted by ORF to steal our identity in Him. We all suffer from an identity crisis to some degree. Our identity was stolen in the Garden of Eden, but Jesus came to restore! Our friend Scott suffered from it, and so he looked to many other things to fulfill what only God can provide.

Peer pressure only has power in an environment where an orphan spirit flourishes. When we know who we are, and "whose" we are, we are not blown about by every wind of doctrine or pressure of this world. We are strong in our walk only when we are strong in whom we are <u>in Him</u>.

Insecurity is a direct result of an orphan spirit. The contrast to that was Jesus; He walked in full confidence of who He was.

If we are not sons, or we see ourselves as orphans, then how can we effectively convey the heart of the Father? We cannot know His love and His heart unless we have experienced it from Him...as a son.

Jesus suffered all things for us. He was no stranger to any of our battles. He could have easily struggled with an orphan spirit since His relationship was set up that way intentionally from the start. He was conceived of the Holy Spirit and not of Joseph, so He grew up in a blended home. Jesus could not be fathered by Joseph in order for us to be established in the heavenly adoption, through Him!

If you look at the way Jesus prayed and compare that to the way we pray, you will see the orphan spirit in probably the starkest contrast of all. Jesus prayed in the Garden of Gethsemane. The Bible tells us that He prayed until the sweat became like great drops of blood.

Luke 22:42-44 [42] saying, "Father, if it is Your will, take this cup away from Me; nevertheless not My will, but Yours, be done." [43] Then an angel appeared to Him from heaven, strengthening Him. [44] And being in agony, He prayed more earnestly. Then His sweat became like great drops of blood falling down to the ground.

My observation of that scripture is that when Jesus prayed, He did so from the heart of a fully trusting Son. He prayed FROM the heart of the Father, not TO the Father.

Jesus told us how to pray the Lord's Prayer:

Matthew 6:8-13 [8] "Therefore do not be like them. For your Father knows the things you have need of before you ask Him. [9] In this manner, therefore, pray:

Our Father in heaven, Hallowed be Your name [10] Your kingdom come. Your will be done on earth as it is in heaven. [11] Give us this day our daily bread. [12] And forgive us our debts, as we forgive our debtors. [13] And do not lead us into temptation, but deliver us from the evil one. For Yours is the kingdom and the power and the glory forever. Amen.

Jesus was all about establishing His Father's Kingdom here on earth, and wants us to be a part of that family.

We should stop praying TO the Father and start praying FROM the Father.

Jesus knew who He was because of the third baptism that He received.

Matthew 3:13-17 *[13] Then Jesus came from Galilee to John at the Jordan to be baptized by him. [14] And John tried to prevent Him, saying, "I need to be baptized by You, and are You coming to me?" [15] But Jesus answered and said to him, "Permit it to be so now, for thus it is fitting for us to fulfill all righteousness." Then he allowed Him. [16] When He had been baptized, Jesus came up immediately from the water; and behold, the heavens were opened to Him, and He saw the Spirit of God descending like a dove and alighting upon Him. [17] And suddenly a voice came from heaven, saying,* **"This is My beloved Son, in whom I am well pleased."**

Jesus was baptized in water, fire (Holy Spirit) and in acceptance as a Son. We are accepted into that same baptism through our belief in Him. We are accepted into the family of God through Jesus.

Galatians 3:26-27 *[26] for you are all sons of God through faith in Christ Jesus. [27] For as many of you as were baptized into Christ have put on Christ.*

That scripture is the main reason I feel that Old Rat Face hates each believer. Not just because we believe in Jesus but because through our belief and faith in Him as our personal Lord and Savior, we **are** sons and daughters. We are already what he will never be, he is an orphan! His desire is to orphan us, to keep us from the promises that are freely given to us through the Cross!

If you don't get anything else from this book, get this, you are <u>already</u> the son/daughter of God through faith in Christ!

You have it. Let your life and prayers declare it. Let go of your kingdom and put on His Kingdom! Put on the desires of the heart of the Father! Your prayers will have power and authority. God did NOT send His Son to establish your kingdom. His was established at Calvary! He took the keys to death and hell. Jesus has it, and we have it, through Him.

1 John 3:7-8 [7] Little children, let no one deceive you. He who practices righteousness is righteous, just as He is righteous. [8] He who sins is of the devil, for the devil has sinned from the beginning. ***For this purpose the Son of God was manifested, that He might destroy the works of the devil.***

The work of ORF was to destroy the cool of the night Garden of Eden experience/relationship with the Father and Jesus did His job to restore it. We just need to walk in it.

Our identities have to be grounded in who we are in Him, or better yet, "whose" we are. If our identity is in other things, we are focused on the wrong kingdom.

I want to preface something before I make my next example or use my next observation. I know a lot of great guys that are into this and they are sold out to Jesus so I am not making a value judgment or a blanket statement.

With that being said, most guys that have gone out and bought a Harley Davidson motorcycle don't stop at just the bike. They need leathers to keep their skin on their body if they ever lay it down on the highway. However it is amazing to me how an accountant can suddenly become an angry, bad dude once he is on that thing. It is comical. They buy the bike and then they need to get the t-shirts, bandanas, and worse yet, the attitude. They feel the need to ride on Sundays instead of going to church...get the point? I have nothing against someone having a bike, corvette, boat, etc. But once your identity becomes a part of that thing, you are walking in an orphan spirit. You become a part of <u>that</u> family or group.

We can do this with social status as well. Watch a person get some money, and suddenly they are a completely different person all together. My point is simple, God did not intend for us to attach our identity to this world but to His. This does NOT however mean that we are to all of a sudden conform to some doctrinal belief of a church either. How we dress or how short or long our hair should be should not matter. It's just not scriptural.

God's desire for us is to be changed from the inside out (our identity) and then use that love and acceptance to go out in the very neighborhoods where we are and change them. I am not telling you to go back into the bars where you hung out before and use that as a reason to fall back into your old ways. NO! I am saying, stop hanging out in the bar. But if you see your old drinking buddy at the grocery store, love on him the same way God loved on you and see what that new identity you have does to him!

I see all kinds of people looking for this adoption process regardless of their faith. Look at Facebook. You have all kinds of people looking to "friend you", but how many of those people are really your friends. It is simply our way of looking for adoption outside of God's plan. Hobbies, gangs, groups, are full of people looking to belong...to a family.

We have such a strong promise in Him that we are NOT orphans, so don't live like one. Don't allow any circumstance or situation to dictate that.

John 14:18 I will not leave you orphans, I will come to you.

Romans 8:14 for as many as are led by the Spirit of God; these are the sons of God.

In Him

Here is a vision I got from the Lord during prayer. I was in Heaven, in the throne room nonetheless, and there was God. On His right side was Jesus, and on Jesus' right side...there I was, seated WITH Christ at the right hand of God and in the throne room! I felt unworthy, like Isaiah or John spoke of, but as I tried to back up (withdraw or cower), Jesus put His arm around me. With His other hand he pulled the arm closest to Him against His side and said..."You belong, you belong in the Fathers house. In ME, you belong".

I belong? In the great throne room of judgment? I belong in the Father's house? In Heaven? Really?

My revelation was that YES, in Him, through Him, we are ALREADY seated with Him at the right hand of the Father! It is all "in Him" and that is our battle cry "in Him". Through our trials, sufferings and temptations we are "in Him".

This redefines our walk as "little Christ's" or Christians as they were referred to in Acts. It takes the relationship to a different level. it makes a book of systematic theology seem, dogmatic and lethargic! This is about relationship, about a new genealogy, a new DNA!

It makes it worth it when our trials and tribulations are not <u>about us</u>! They are for us to learn from and take to others. To lead others to the One that ultimately suffered all for us!

All I can say is...Wow!

Chapter 6

Trust

Writing this book has definitely been an interesting journey. I have realized the orphan spirit manifestations so many times in my own life, and quite frankly, it has been alarming to me to see how messed up I really am.

The whole process of learning how to publish a book, the inner turmoil of questioning the material and just dealing with the day to day mental gymnastics of "did God really say" has caused me to realize that trust is a core topic and an orphan issue that I see paralyzing not only me, but the entire body of Christ. As a believer we have to walk daily in trust to a certain level, but overall, we all struggle to live up to its full calling, or better yet, the full potential it could have in our lives.

We are all guilty of wanting to see a "sign" like Gideon did. We all struggle with trusting what the Father tells us. It manifests through deep seated fears of "do I really hear from God" or even the oldest trick in the book, "did God really say".

God spoke to Gideon in *Judges 6:14 The Lord turned to him and said, go in this might of yours, and you shall save Israel form the hand of the Midianites. Have I not sent you?*

Gideon was a weak man in his own eyes and didn't walk or talk like a man who was a mighty man, regardless of what the Lord said.

Judges 6:12 and the angel of the Lord appeared to him and said to him, the Lord is with you, you mighty man of valor!

Gideon, in his amazing child-like faith (I am kidding here) wanted the Lord to prove Himself, so he would be sure what the Lord wanted him to do. We all struggle with this issue. We all question whether or not we have heard from God, but this was not the issue with Gideon. He was paralyzed by an orphan spirit that made him question if God *really, really* wanted to use **him** for **His** purpose. I've been there. I have looked in the mirror and wondered if I was really worthy to be called by God. If God really said that to me. If God really wanted to use me in such a mighty way. (Example-this book!)

God gave us this story in Judges 6 for our benefit, not so that we can imitate it, but so we can see what NOT to do. God is patient with Gideon, answers his prayers and reveals Himself to Gideon. But when is it enough? When do you just take a step of faith…by the way, that requires YOU take the step. When do you just go into whatever He is calling you to and just do it?

Yet somehow, we all still get suckered into a walk like Gideon's where we are so unsure of ourselves and who we are in Him, that we want God to perform some miraculous "trick" or act in order for us to follow His desires for our life. Where is the faith in that? Why do we always want Him to provide us with tangible proof when it says in Hebrews that faith is in the **not** seen?

Hebrews 11 [1] Now faith is the substance of things hoped for, the evidence of things not seen.

I have seen this orphan/trust issue manifested in my walk with Him definitely more during the time of writing this book and all that entails, not to mention the stepping out in faith of researching and publishing it as well. I have had the inner gymnastics of questioning whether this was really God, why me, did God really say to do this, etc. The Lord has remained faithful in being patient with me and allowing me to work <u>through</u> this "with" Him. His desire is to bless me, not put a burden on me.

Jeremiah 17:5-10 [5] *Thus says the LORD: "Cursed is the man who trusts in man and makes flesh his strength, whose heart departs from the LORD.* [6] *For he shall be like a shrub in the desert, And shall not see when good comes, But shall inhabit the parched places in the wilderness, In a salt land which is not inhabited.* [7] *"Blessed is the man who trusts in the LORD, and whose hope is the LORD.* [8] *For he shall be like a tree planted by the waters, Which spreads out its roots by the river, And will not fear when heat comes; But its leaf will be green, And will not be anxious in the year of drought, Nor will cease from yielding fruit.* [9] *"The heart is deceitful above all things, And desperately wicked; Who can know it?* [10] *I, the LORD, search the heart, I test the mind, Even to give every man according to his ways, According to the fruit of his doings.*

I realized that to truly walk in the faith that God desired for me, I had to camp out on this scripture and make it more than just a Bible verse; I had to make it mine! Jesus also said that His yoke was easy and burden was light, yet you wouldn't know it from my walk! You would have thought at times that I was all alone, out in the wilderness, in the enemies camp, with only a butter knife and a loin cloth to single handedly defend and serve the Lord my God against the entire world!

The truth is that I am not alone, and God has said multiple times that He would never leave me nor forsake me.

Hebrews 13:5 let your conduct be without covetousness; be content with such things as you have. For He Himself has said, **"I will never leave you nor forsake you."**

Deut 31:6 be strong and of good courage, do not fear nor be afraid of them for the Lord your God, He is the One who goes with you. **He will never leave nor forsake you.**

Joshua 1:5 No man shall be able to stand before you all the days of your life; as I was with Moses, so will I be with you, **I will not leave you nor forsake you.**

Do we need any more proof? Since the Father does not lie, wouldn't it make sense then that a lack of trust in what He has said is your issue. We struggle with trust because of a lack of intimacy, or a lacking in our relationship and knowledge of the Father's heart concerning us.

A lack of trust is a sign of an orphan spirit.

Our Father doesn't ever put us in a place of harm or intentional pain for His enjoyment or amusement. His desire is *for* you and to complete you through the trials and challenges of this life. He wants us to "know" Him in the most intimate of ways. Let me explain.

Hosea 4:6 My people are destroyed for lack of knowledge. Because you have rejected knowledge,

I studied this scripture a while back because it really intrigued me. Was God saying that the stupid people are the ones that will be destroyed? That seemed a little unfair to me since He created them, so if they are stupid it is His fault. However, you cannot take this scripture at just the face value of the English translation, since the Greek and Hebrew languages are much more colorful and thus a translation to English sometimes leaves out the true meaning. I mentioned in the beginning of the book that even though the orphan spirit is not written in black and white of the Bible, the Lord sees it and desires us to be free of it.

The knowing that the Bible speaks of in this Hosea verse is not just the Webster's Dictionary meaning of:

(know) Verb/nō/
1. Be aware of through observation, inquiry, or information.
2. Have knowledge or information concerning

We cannot stop at just our surface level understanding, otherwise we will miss the bigger picture. Just knowing "about" God will NOT save you.

James 2:19 [19] You believe that there is one God. You do well. Even the demons believe—and tremble!

Let's go back to Hosea and study this passage even deeper. The word used for "knowledge" is the Hebrew word H1847 Da'ath and that is from a root word H3045 Yada, (hang in there this gets good). If we study the word Yada we will see multiple times in scripture where it is used and it simply means a serious act of intimacy.

Genesis 4:1 Now Adam knew Eve his wife, and she conceived and bore Cain. When Adam "knew" Eve, they bore a son, it is the same word Yada. Let's go back to that passage in Hosea and re-read it with a more colorful definition.

My people are destroyed because they didn't desire intimacy with Me, and because they reject My intimacy, the very lifeblood they need to survive they will be destroyed.

That is my translation (the JVV, Jon Voyles version) of that passage. Outside of an intimate relationship with Him, there is NO life!

It is the same message we have been given in *John 14:6 ⁶ Jesus said to him, "I am the way, the truth, and the life. No one comes to the Father except through Me.* We simply cannot get there any other way.

You have to take the sexuality and sensuality out of this. The Lord created us for intimacy, and desires the deepest spiritual intimacy we can possibly have with Him. He is not interested in a physical relationship here, but a spiritual connection.

It is His desire to know us and for us to know Him. We will be destroyed without it!

God is not bent on destroying stupid people! (Can I get a Amen and thank you Jesus!) He is interested in taking ordinary people that are not walking in a life of intimacy with Him, and drawing them into His home and becoming "one" in the spirit.

When Adam "knew" Eve in order to bring about Cain or Abel, they had to become one in the flesh. Through that act of becoming one they had also created one flesh in their child (2 people's DNA, creating 1 new person). That is what the Lord is looking to do with you in the spirit realm, to become a new creation!

In today's society, especially in the United States, we have a very flippant attitude towards sex and its desired intention by the Creator, and it directly affects our relationship with Him. I feel that when two people enter into that kind of relationship, whether they realize it or not, they are entering into a spiritual connection too. That may be why a person that has had multiple partners has such a hard time getting into a truly connected relationship with someone. There is no line in the sand. There is no boundary to work with. They have connected with others to the point that they don't know who they are, let alone "whose" they are.

That is as deep as I want to go with that explanation because as important as that is for us to understand, we are getting off track from this chapter. If you can follow my thought pattern, God's desire is for us to have a "non-sexual, non-sensual" spiritual intimacy with Him that will connect us and make us one. How can we "know" when He is talking to us, if we don't "know" the One who is talking?

Without intimacy, truly "knowing" Him, we cannot trust Him. Without trusting Him, we cannot step out in the fullness of His calling "in Him".

When we step out in faith and walk according to His desire, and not according to our circumstances or fears, we can accomplish anything. We can walk on water. We can heal the sick. We can write books. ☺

When we walk in fear of any kind, we are not walking according to faith. If we are not walking according to faith, we have no trust. If we have no trust, it is because we have lacked the intimate time with our Daddy God to get His heart and hear His thoughts.

I have learned that in **all** things I should give thanks and to be transparent. It has been what has set me free in my own walk and it is my prayer that you are set free as well.

Chapter 7

Victim Mentality

The orphan spirit will reveal itself through a victim mentality. A victim is someone who wants to tell everyone how they are not being treated fairly, how life has dealt them a bad hand or that they are not blessed as others are. This is an orphan; they want to defend themselves through creating circumstantial evidence to get someone else's sympathy. That sympathy is usually feeding a spirit that "masks" itself to keep that person from seeing their own shortcoming and dealing with the shortcoming through repentance and chastisement from God. God wants to complete us and uses the situations of this world in order to do that.

It is interesting how you can have two identical situations that produce two completely different results or paradigms. One person claims that they were not equipped properly to deal with the situation (that God dealt them a bad hand). The other person deals with life and moves on.

One of them embraces the circumstances and uses it to complete and build them up. The other will not embrace it, and deal with it in a negative manner. They will refuse to see that they are a part of the problem rather than a victim of the circumstance.

My point is that an orphan will use the circumstances to defend their position in life, and to charge a faithful God with unfaithfulness. Was it fair that I was hit by a semi traveling at 55MPH that caused me numerous injuries and pain that I still live with daily? No it wasn't, but I am SO THANKFUL that life is not fair!

If life was fair then Jesus would not have had to suffer on the Cross for our sins!

You would have to pay the penalty for your own sins if life were fair, so it would do you some good to stop the belly aching about how God has dealt you this unfair hand.

Play the hand you are dealt!

James 1:2-4 **²** *My brethren, count it all joy when you fall into various trials,* **³** *knowing that the testing of your faith produces patience.* **⁴** *But let patience have its perfect work, that you may be perfect and complete, lacking nothing.*

There is an amazing transformation that happens in a person's life when you stop living like an orphan and blaming everything on an "unfair God". You will come to the realization that God will use all of the challenges of this life to build you up, to complete you. He will make you into someone that you never knew you could be. His intent is to build up, His heart is to complete.

Stop fighting Him and embrace Him.

If you are truly a victim, then this passage of scripture is a lie. If any part of the Bible is a lie, then it is all a lie and we are all doomed!

Romans 8:37-39 **³⁷** *Yet in all these things we are more than conquerors through Him who loved us.* **³⁸** *For I am persuaded* *that neither death nor life, nor angels nor principalities nor powers, nor things present nor things to come, [39] nor height nor depth, nor any other created thing, shall be able to separate us from the love of God which is in Christ Jesus our Lord.*

More than conquerors! Does that apply to your life, or are you not His child? Nothing can or will separate us from the love of God which is in Christ Jesus our Lord, so stop trying to find something! By adopting an orphan spirit, you are "kicking against the goads" and fighting the very infallible Word of God. It would do you good to embrace the truth!

Here is a comment that I hear all the time from victims/orphans: "Why do bad things happen to good people"? This is an interesting comment that some have taken ownership of and walk in. Let's start with the basis of this lie, (yes it is a lie) good and bad.

To start with, who are we to determine what is good and what is bad? Let's go the very core of Christianity to tackle this subject. Was what happened at the Cross good or bad? Good for you! Bad for sin! So was that a bad thing that happened to Jesus or good? If you think that it was a bad thing that happened to Jesus then explain this scripture to me.

John 16:20 [20] Most assuredly, I say to you that you will weep and lament, but the world will rejoice; and you will be sorrowful, but your sorrow will be turned into joy.

To the disciples it appeared to be a bad thing that Jesus would have to endure the Cross. I have seen the Passion of Christ. It didn't appear to be a good thing when it was happening! Even the disciples ran away because it appeared to be bad. Did the disciples sit around complaining about how they could not believe how such a bad thing happened to such a good man? We now know differently, we know that the Cross was a good thing! We cannot take the circumstance and weigh it at face value.

*Hebrews 12:2 ² looking unto Jesus, the author and finisher of our faith, who **for the joy that was set before Him endured the cross**, despising the shame, and has sat down at the right hand of the throne of God.*

The JOY? Really?

1 Corinthians 1:18 ¹⁸ For the message of the cross is foolishness to those who are perishing, but to us who are being saved it is the power of God.

We should stop trying to tell God what is good and bad. That is an orphan speaking, someone who doesn't know, trust or understand the heart of their Father.

Why do we charge a good God with bad things?

If that isn't enough scripture and thoughts to help you to realize where the victim mentality comes from, I am not sure what I can do to convince you. Was what Jesus endured for you enough? If not, there is no hope.

You are more than conquerors **through Him**. Stop believing the orphan spirit lies and embrace walking in the fullness of being a son!

Chapter 8

Revenge & Judgment

Revenge is a manifestation of the orphan spirit in a situation where you don't trust that God will defend you properly; you would rather get your own revenge. You don't trust that God will do a good enough job against your enemy. You know more than God about what needs to be done to them in order for the punishment to equal the crime.

You simply don't trust God and His Word for that. You are struggling with unforgiveness towards whoever hurt you and you make comments like "You don't know what that person did to me". But God does! He knows what is going on and has it completely under control.

Revenge is probably the ugliest of all the orphan fruits. It will destroy the person that eats of it, yet make that person feel like they are benefiting from eating of it, so they eat more. Look at Hollywood for example. There are many movies out there that focus on revenge and getting even for someone who has been wronged. It fuels a perverted sense of judgment that can really cause someone a lot of internal harm.

Are you sure you want to open up that cage? For instance, what if God never intervened on YOUR behalf for something that <u>you did</u> to someone else? It could be something as simple as cutting someone off in traffic or breaking up with a girlfriend. It could be much worse, especially if you have walked according the fleshly desires of this world. There are many sins in my life that I am extremely thankful that God didn't allow another person to have justified revenge on me. I deserved it, but God had other plans, to use my sin and shortcoming in order to bring about something in my life that would produce life, not death.

I am sure that if you were to think long enough you would find areas where you would be thankful as well. So why don't we all put down our rocks before someone's glass house get a busted window!

Romans 12:19-21 [19] *Beloved, do not avenge yourselves, but rather give place to wrath; for it is written,* **"Vengeance is Mine, I will repay" says the Lord.** [20] *Therefore "If your enemy is hungry, feed him; If he is thirsty, give him a drink; For in so doing you will heap coals of fire on his head."* [21] **Do not be overcome by evil, but overcome evil with good.**

You judge only because you don't know the righteous Judge! You take those matters into your own hands because of a lack of relationship and trust in your Dad!

2 Timothy 4:8 [8] *Finally, there is laid up for me the crown of righteousness, which the Lord,* **the righteous Judge,** *will give to me on that Day, and* **not to me only but also to all** *who have loved His appearing.*

God is faithful and a righteous judge who is no respecter of persons, those that need judgment and those who what to inflict it. Think about this the next time you deserve judgment. Use the same love, mercy and forgiveness that you were so freely given. I am NOT saying it is easy, but it IS scriptural and the only thing that brings forth life.

Chapter 9

Passivity

Here is a tricky manifestation of the orphan spirit, passivity. When we don't trust that God will come through, sometimes we will do nothing. I believe there is a time for us to "be still and know that He is God", but that is not what we are talking about. We are talking about someone that is either worn out or just doesn't care anymore, and refuses to pick up their sword to go into battle. This happens when we disassociate ourselves from God. We adopt an orphan spirit in any situation where we perceive we are already defeated.

When you have a defeated attitude and refuse to protect your family in prayer, it is extremely destructive. Think about a country that refuses to fight. They are not much of a challenge. You just mow them over and take what you want.

Proverbs 24:30 ^{30} I went by the field of the lazy man, And by the vineyard of the man devoid of understanding; ^{31} And there it was, all overgrown with thorns; Its surface was covered with nettles; Its stone wall was broken down. ^{32} When I saw it, I considered it well; I looked on it and received instruction: ^{33} A little sleep, a little slumber, A little folding of the hands to rest;^{34} So shall your poverty come like a prowler, And your need like an armed man.

God does NOT want us to be passive nor defeated. In Jesus we have already won, we need to take what is ours! We have got to step into the armor he has for us and wage the war that is ours to fight!

I know the next passage is somewhat lengthy but it has been a blessing for me to read time and time again. When you read this, please think of it from the stand point of an intercessor or watchman. The Lord will anoint us to see what is coming and how to defend against it! We are a part of His Kingdom, are His kids. He desires for us to be warriors and watchmen in His name, for His Kingdom.

Ezekiel 33:1-11 **¹** *Again the word of the LORD came to me, saying,* **²** *"Son of man, speak to the children of your people, and say to them: 'When I bring the sword upon a land, and the people of the land take a man from their territory and make him their watchman,* **³** *when he sees the sword coming upon the land, if he blows the trumpet and warns the people,* **⁴** *then whoever hears the sound of the trumpet and does not take warning, if the sword comes and takes him away, his blood shall be on his own head.* **⁵** *He heard the sound of the trumpet, but did not take warning; his blood shall be upon himself. But he who takes warning will save his life.* **⁶** *But if the watchman sees the sword coming and does not blow the trumpet, and the people are not warned, and the sword comes and takes any person from among them, he is taken away in his iniquity; but his blood I will require at the watchman's hand.'* **⁷** *"So you, son of man: I have made you a watchman for the house of Israel; therefore you shall hear a word from My mouth and warn them for Me.* **⁸** *When I say to the wicked, 'O wicked man, you shall surely die!' and you do not speak to warn the wicked from his way, that wicked man shall die in his iniquity; but his blood I will require at your hand.* **⁹** *Nevertheless if you warn the wicked to turn from his way, and he does not turn from his way, he shall die in his iniquity; but you have delivered your soul.* **¹⁰** *"Therefore you, O son of man, say to the house of Israel: 'Thus you say, "If our transgressions and our sins lie upon us,* *and we pine away in them, how can we then live?"'* ¹¹ *Say to them: 'As I live,' says the Lord GOD, 'I have no pleasure in the death of the wicked, but that the wicked turn from his way and live. Turn, turn from your evil ways! For why should you die, O house of Israel?'*

It is our responsibility to watch and pray; our responsibility to take action as the Lord directs. As that passage just stated, if we do not intercede, the blood of that person is on your head! Passivity is extremely destructive.

When someone walks in a spirit of passivity, it is because they don't know who their Dad is? A God of War, a Warrior, a Victorious King! Step up and take the position of a warrior for Christ! It is YOUR lineage! Your DNA!

Chapter 10

Hope Deferred

Delayed promises are one of the easiest areas that can cause you to pick up an orphan spirit. It comes when something that you believe God for, or are hoping for, doesn't happen or is postponed. You can quickly pick up an offense with God because you believed, as He said to, and that something (whatever it is) doesn't come to pass as you expected.

Do you realize that waiting is a verb, an action word? If it were a noun we could sit idly by on the posterior portions of our physical anatomies and watch the world go by as we wait.

Waiting on God should be something that we are "leaning into".

A runner waiting to start a race doesn't take a position of leaning against the fence by the bleachers, smoking a cigarette, talking with his friends or texting his girlfriend. He is in the starting blocks, intensely anticipating the sound of the starter pistol. Can that be said about your walk with God? Would God say that you are eagerly waiting? Actively waiting is a sign of someone who has faith...in Him, not the circumstances.

David waited for a long time for his promise to be fulfilled as the King of Israel. He not only had to wait, but he had to defend himself for the very cause of God. His heart had to remain focused on what God said and not on the circumstances surrounding him daily.

Let's go back to our old buddy Scott. He was hoping in the sale of the copier so that he could take his family on that trip to Florida. Was the hope that he had in the sale of the copier, as well as the trip, a hope that was placed in him by God, or was it something that he just hoped would happen? Was it to make his wife and kids happy? His heart may have been in the right place. Some may say that he truly wanted to bless his family. It is interesting to see however, just how God will use things like this to get our attention, to reveal the true condition of our hearts.

Proverbs 13:12 **12** *Hope deferred make the heart sick, but a longing fulfilled is a tree of life.*

I meditated over that scripture for some time before I felt that I understood what the Lord wanted me to see. His question for me was, "Is your heart sick, are you frustrated, and at the end of your rope? Look inward to what your hope is actually in. Is your hope in what the Lord has given you? Or is your hope in the desires of your own flesh?"

This got me thinking, and searching.

Psalm 37:4 **4** *delight yourself also in the LORD, and He shall give you the desires of your heart.*

That verse can be, and is often, very misleading if taken out of context. We all too often use the name of Jesus in our prayers as a way to manipulate God to agree with what WE want, not necessarily what is best for us or what He wants. We will even remind Him of His Word in order to twist His arm!

We delight ourselves in our desires all too often.

What I feel this verse is really saying is that when you make Him your delight, He will put His desire in you, and that desire then becomes your desire.

John 15:7-8 ⁷ If you abide in Me, and My words abide in you, you will ask what you desire, and it shall be done for you. ⁸ By this My Father is glorified, that you bear much fruit; so you will be My disciples.

If we are IN Him, then we line up our hearts with His heart and we can ask what we desire, (His will) and we are promised that our prayers will be answered.

*1 John 5:14-15 ¹⁴ Now this is the confidence that we have in Him, that if we ask anything **according to His will**, He hears us. ¹⁵ And if we know that He hears us, whatever we ask, we know that we have the petitions that we have asked of Him.*

He allows us to fail in our prayers so that we can discover what is best for us, His plan. In the 1 John 5:14 verse, I realized that if I am not asking according to His will, I have no confidence in that He even hears my prayers. He doesn't hear all the wish list stuff that I petition Him for. If we gave our kids everything they asked for we would be bankrupt and have nowhere to put all the junk!

God knows what is best for us, we really don't. We think we do, but that is the orphan talking. His desire is to bring us into a relationship with Him that is not predicated on what He gives us or on our attitude if we don't get what we want. It may be that the hope deferred in your life is what is making you sick. Take it to the Cross to get the tree of life, Him!

Dad knows what you need, and when you need it!

Chapter 11

What are you so afraid of?

That was the question God posed to me when I went on a walk with Him one beautiful August morning. I wasn't sure exactly what I was afraid of, but there was fear and it was obvious, because I was praying, "to" Him instead of "from" Him. I knew that there was an underlying issue, and Dad wanted to do some surgery on my heart.

Some background information of my life would be helpful in understanding this chapter. I'm self-employed, as a financial service professional; I have been self-employed since the 90's, so that is nothing new. What has happened over the course of the last few years has put me in a place that has been rather uncomfortable. There has been a series of challenges that have come my way and because of them I have learned to trust Him more, way more.

The economy has hurt us all so that is not as much of an issue as you would think. However over the last 4 years my wife and I have had some experiences that caused us to really seek Him or choose to run away. I know there is no life in running away from Him, so that wasn't really an option. Not to mention, since He is omnipresent, how do I run away?

In the last 4 years, my wife and I have both had to undergo major surgery; I was in a wheel chair for a portion of 2009, and the result was medical bills up the wazoo! Trust me that is the last place you want medical bills. ☺

I also got into a partnership that failed, miserably. I had to rebuild my business from scratch and blew through my savings just trying to survive.

Let's go back to my walk with God. I thought about what He had asked me for a few minutes and He showed me what some of my fears were:

- I was a self-employed person!
- I was afraid of failing.
- Being able to pay my mortgage.
- To be ashamed in front of my peers.
- What my family would think?
- What my neighbors would think?
- Etc...

God's answer was short and clear; "Was Jesus concerned with any of this?" OUCH! I realized that Jesus was not afraid or even concerned about this world; He had an understanding of the words spoken by God.

Matt 3:17 This is my beloved son of whom I am well pleased.

Jesus was not concerned with the cares of this world. Jesus was so heavenly minded that He was no earthly good. He focused solely on the Father's desires and about bringing His Father's Kingdom to earth. He was good for us, but to the earthly kingdom of realm and sin, He was no earthly good.

The point is simple, we all are focusing on the things of this kingdom and putting our trust in them and not ACTIVELY pursuing the things that our Abba Father would have us focus on. We put our trust in chariots and horses, or man.

Psalm 146:3-4 do not put your trust in princes nor in a son of man in whom there is no help. His spirit departs, he returns to his earth, that day his very plans perish.

Psalm 20:7 some trust in chariots and some in horses but we will remember the Lord our God.

When we truly know that we are sons of the Almighty God and not orphans, then we do not strive to become something that we are not. We do not concern ourselves with earthly issues, nor do we get our trust wrapped around something temporal. Like our fictional friend Scott, I have had my focus on this kingdom for way too long. Does that mean I will not be diligent to do my work or have a complacent flippant attitude? No, actually just the opposite. I will do things with excellence **because** of the Kingdom that I represent. I do NOT want to bring shame to my Father.

Proverbs 10:1 A wise son makes a glad father. My desire is to make my Dad glad!

What a representation that obliterates the orphan spirit. My Dad knows where I am at. He knows what I need. If I am to walk in my Father's will, I need to be close to hear Him. I want to please my Dad. I want to strive for excellence, not perfection... only one of those is attainable!

We can all hear from the Father. We can get our marching orders....from Dad. There is no disconnect because the kingdom is within us! We already have it as believers in Christ Jesus!

We need not worry nor even be concerned with anything of this world other than what the Father tells us to.

Apparently I am not a quick learner because here I am again, a few weeks later, in prayer for my business and finances. I wanted a breakthrough and was going to diligently seek His face until I got it...sometimes I think God laughs at me.

A few weeks later, I am headed in my car to an appointment and here I am praying, again for my business. (Told you I am not a quick learner) I am complaining about finances, asking for that "breakthrough". God said again to me, "What's the matter son? Are you tired of being in My bosom?" OUCH!

He then gave me another vision regarding this. I am sitting on the Father's lap and as He held me there He said; "Orphans don't get to do this, only sons do." As this was happening, there were all kinds of things going on around us (good and bad, both the worship and the worry), the Father said; "Don't pay any attention to any of that, I am taking care of it **all**."

It was a picture of what redemption is supposed to be, redeeming the right relationship with the Father. It is what He wanted from the beginning in the Garden of Eden. He isn't as concerned as we are about our goals, cars, homes, or even our church. He wants to redeem our relationship with Him.

What He said to me about this vision is; "This is MY desire, this is what I want from ALL my kids, lap time".

Immediately following that vision, there was another vision that followed of a 3 year old sitting on his dad's lap squirming around, trying to get down and get into trouble, then a picture of that same child asleep in his father's arms. It represented peace in His arms in spite of the circumstances. That is the heart of the Father for all of us.

God showed me that it is fun to be on His lap. The view is much better up there. His desire is to show us what He sees, and from there we can walk as Jesus did.

From the Fathers lap, Jesus was able to forgive instantly even in the face of crucifixion, He trusted His Dad.

Luke 23:34 ³⁴ Then Jesus said, "Father, forgive them, for they do not know what they do."

From the lap of our Father we can see as He sees and we can get our marching orders <u>from</u> Him. It is in that time we can pray prayers that are from His heart. And we can know His thoughts.

Jeremiah 29:11 ¹¹ For I know the thoughts that I think toward you, says the LORD, thoughts of peace and not of evil, to give you a future and a hope.

We don't know the plans, but HE does.

His heart is for me <u>as a son</u>, why don't I see that? The Father said He would never leave me or forsake me.

Hebrews 13:5 Let your conduct be without covetousness; be content with such things as you have. For He Himself has said, "I will never leave you nor forsake you."

Deuteronomy 31:6 Be strong and of good courage, do not fear nor be afraid of them for the Lord your God, He is the One who goes with you. **He will never leave nor forsake you.**

Joshua 1:5 No man shall be able to stand before you all the days of your life; as I was with Moses, so will I be with you, **I will not leave you nor forsake you.**

I know that I have used those scriptures in previous chapters, but we are not acting like children who understand that Dad cannot lie.

Numbers 23:19 **¹⁹** **"God is not a man, that He should lie**, *Nor a son of man, that He should repent Has He said, and will He not do? Or has He spoken, and will He not make it good?*

Romans 3:4 **⁴** *Certainly not! Indeed, let* **God be true** *but every man a liar.*

Titus 1:2 **²** *in hope of eternal life which* **God, who cannot lie**, *promised before time began*

We charge God with unfaithfulness all the time; anytime we don't believe Him we are calling Him a liar!

Mark 4:35-40 **³⁵** *On the same day, when evening had come, He said to them, "Let us cross over to the other side."* **³⁶** *Now when they had left the multitude, they took Him along in the boat as He was. And other little boats were also with Him.* **³⁷** *And a great windstorm arose, and the waves beat into the boat, so that it was already filling.* **³⁸** *But He was in the stern, asleep on a pillow. And they awoke Him and said to Him, "Teacher, do You not care that we are perishing?"* **³⁹** *Then He arose and rebuked the wind, and said to the sea, "Peace, be still!" And the wind ceased and there was a great calm.* **⁴⁰** *But He said to them, "Why are you so fearful? How is it that you have no faith?"*

Jesus spoke the truth to the disciples when He said they would cross over to the other side. However, the disciples operated in an orphan sprit by waking Him as if to say, "Don't you see my storm? Don't you care what is going to happen to me?"

We have Jesus in our boat too, so before we can judge them, we should look at our own actions and speech. Is our walk predicated on the hope and faith in the truth of His promises? Or has it become a position of telling God all about your storm?

Jesus told the disciples that they would go over to the other side! They felt it was their responsibility to wake up the Son of God, to cry out for their plight…some of us do the same:

- God You don't understand?
- God can't You see what's going on?
- Don't You care?

Sounds like an orphan that doesn't believe he is a son! Jesus is WITH us. He said He would never leave us, do you believe it? Do you trust Him? Can you see the path?

Isaiah 42:16 [16] *I will bring the blind by a way they did not know; I will lead them in paths they have not known. I will make darkness light before them, and crooked places straight. These things I will do for them, and not forsake them.*

He can! We are in His bosom and what an awesome place to be! Are we above Him? Are we too big to sit in Abba Father's lap? God I hope I am NEVER too big for Your lap!

Here is His promise:

Isaiah 54:17 ¹⁷No weapon formed against you shall prosper, And every tongue which rises against you in judgment You shall condemn. This is the heritage of the servants of the LORD, And their righteousness is from Me," Says the LORD.

Are you a servant? Then this is <u>your</u> promise.

Another orphan comment that I have heard spoken all too often is "the Lord helps those who help themselves". Let me ask you, where is that in the Bible? Is it in the Bible? NO, it is in Benjamin Franklin's "Poor Richard's Almanac". Actually the Bible says something completely different.

Psalm 28:6-8 Blessed be the Lord, because He has heard the voice of my supplications! The Lord is my strength and my shield; **<u>My heart trusted in Him and I am helped;</u>** *Therefore my heart greatly rejoices and with my song I will praise Him. The Lord is their strength and He is the saving refuge of His anointed.*

By trusting in Him, and not ourselves, we are helped. We are NOT orphaned by the Father. We are accepted. We are approved. We are sons (and daughters). The heart of the Father is for us to be one with Him.

It is not about works, feelings, and emotions. It is about being a son not an orphan. The bride and bridegroom are one.

Here is a question for you, can you be almost a son? You are either a son or you are not. Can you be almost pregnant?

You are pregnant or you are not. Can you be almost saved? You are either saved or you are not. There is NO middle ground here; it is strictly black or white.

When we trust in anything other than God, or we listen to anything other than the shepherd, we won't walk like His sheep.

It really is that simple, what are you so afraid of?

Chapter 12

Affliction is the mark of a son

This is probably the most conflicting of all the fruits of an orphan spirit. Affliction will cause us to do many things, and probably the most common of all is to withdraw. We will shrink back when the going gets tough. We don't realize that in order for us to walk as sons, <u>we must suffer</u> in the same way as Jesus, God's only son that has brought us to the family through adoption.

2 Corinthians 1:3-7 ³ Blessed be the God and Father of our Lord Jesus Christ, the Father of mercies and God of all comfort, ⁴ who comforts us in all our tribulation, that we may be able to comfort those who are in any trouble, with the comfort with which we ourselves are comforted by God. ⁵ For as the sufferings of Christ abound in us, so our consolation also abounds through Christ. ⁶ Now if we are afflicted, it is for your consolation and salvation, which is effective for enduring the same sufferings which we also suffer. Or if we are comforted, it is for your consolation and salvation. ⁷ And our hope for you is steadfast, because we know that as you are partakers of the sufferings, so also you will partake of the consolation.

Why are we afflicted as sons? Verse 4 gives us insight to that reason; we are afflicted for others. To show others the comfort which we are given from God. If there were no troubles or trials, we would have no need for God. We can claim to serve and follow Him, but it is when the furnace is turned up 7 times hotter than normal that our faith is tested. In verse 7 it states that without the suffering we cannot partake of the consolation. I have heard others say, the harsher the battle, the sweeter the victory.

My faith has been tried through affliction many times. Sometimes I have passed, and sometimes I have failed miserably. Nonetheless, God has been, and remains faithful in my life, regardless of the affliction. It is because of those times of hardship and trials that I have sought Him more.

Matthew 7:13-14 Enter by the narrow gate; for wide is the gate and broad is the way that leads to destruction and there are many who go in by it. Because narrow is the gate and ***difficult is the way that leads to life*** *and there are few who find it.*

Few find it because we spend most of our time avoiding it. God wants us to be sons, why should we think we are greater than Jesus and that we should not have to deal with affliction? Is the servant greater than the Master? Where in the Bible does it state that because of the cross we will be without struggle? It says just the opposite, that the rain falls on the just and unjust alike. Jesus said to expect to be hated just as he was hated.

We accepted Him and we have become Christians or "little Christ's" as they were referred to in Acts.

1 Peter 1:6-12 In this you greatly rejoice, though now for a little while, if need be, you have been grieved by various trials, that the genuineness of your faith, being much more precious that gold that perishes, though it is tested by fire, may be found to praise, honor and glory at the revelation of Jesus Christ, whom having not seen you love. Though now you do not see Him, yet believing, you rejoice with joy inexpressible and full of glory, receiving the end of your faith—the salvation of your souls. Of this salvation the prophets have inquired and searched carefully, who prophesied of the grace that would come to you, searching what, or what manner of time, the Spirit of Christ who was in them was indicating when He testified beforehand the sufferings of Christ and the glories that would follow. To them it was revealed that, not to themselves, but to us they were ministering the things which now have reported to you through those who have preached the gospel to you by the Holy Spirit sent from heaven—things which angels desire to look into.

Heb 2:10 for it was fitting for Him, for whom are all things and by whom are all things, in bringing many sons to glory, to make the captain of their salvation perfect <u>through</u> sufferings.

We are sons; we suffer WITH Him for His glory. We need to accept the hardships knowing that our God is a faithful God and judges righteously. Our afflictions and hardships are not punishment, but permanent markings that identify us as His!

Romans 8:16-17 **¹⁶** *The Spirit Himself bears witness with our spirit that we are children of God,* **¹⁷** *and if children, then heirs—heirs of God and joint heirs with Christ,* ***if indeed we suffer with Him****, that we may also be glorified together.*

We suffer WITH Him; we will be glorified together, but we have to suffer in order for the glory to come. That mark of a son is like a tattoo. They are permanent and they hurt!

Affliction is the mark of a son!

Our affliction is for His glory, for Him to be revealed in this time.

John 9:1-3 ¹ Now as Jesus passed by, He saw a man who was blind from birth. ² And His disciples asked Him, saying, "Rabbi, who sinned, this man or his parents, that he was born blind?" ³ Jesus answered, "Neither this man nor his parents sinned, but that the works of God should be revealed in him.

It may be that we don't understand that afflictions as well as punishment are expressions of love. They will cause us to feel orphaned until we understand the heart of a Father that loves us too much to allow us to stay in the funk that we live in every day.

Proverbs 3:11-12 "my son, do not despise the chastening of the Lord, nor detest His correction: For whom the Lord loves he corrects, just as the father the son in whom he delights."

In whom He delights. I could be wrong but that sounds like a Dad that wants the best for His son and will not allow him to follow his folly. I have disciplined my kids a lot and never once did I do it for MY benefit.

We look at affliction as a bad thing, but without the affliction of the blind man, the disciples would not been able to see the works of God. Think about Meshach, Shadrach, & Abednego. It was in their affliction that their faith and trust in God was tested, tried and proven.

Daniel 3:19-23 ¹⁹ Then Nebuchadnezzar was full of fury, and the expression on his face changed toward Shadrach, Meshach, and Abednego. He spoke and commanded that they heat the furnace seven times more than it was usually heated. ²⁰ And he commanded certain mighty men of valor who were in his army to bind Shadrach, Meshach, and Abednego, and cast them into the burning fiery furnace.

²¹ Then these men were bound in their coats, their trousers, their turbans, and their other garments, and were cast into the midst of the burning fiery furnace. ²² Therefore, because the king's command was urgent, and the furnace exceedingly hot, the flame of the fire killed those men who took up Shadrach, Meshach, and Abednego. ²³ And these three men, Shadrach, Meshach, and Abednego, fell down bound into the midst of the burning fiery furnace..

A fire that was set 7 times hotter than normal? I don't know what normal is, but that sounds hot! A fire that was so hot in fact, that those who threw them in died.

That is some serious affliction, and we all benefit from their trial. It gives us hope.

Trust in Him, knowing that He loves His sons and His desire is to complete them, not to harm them!

Look at another patriarch of our faith, Paul. Aside from Jesus, no one I know of has suffered more than him for the cause of Christ. Here is what the Lord spoke concerning Paul to Ananias after the Damascus Road experience.

*Acts 9:13-16 ¹³ Then Ananias answered, "Lord, I have heard from many about this man, how much harm he has done to Your saints in Jerusalem. ¹⁴ And here he has authority from the chief priests to bind all who call on Your name." ¹⁵ But the Lord said to him, "Go, for he is a chosen vessel of Mine to bear My name before Gentiles, kings, and the children of Israel. ¹⁶ **For I will show him how many things he must suffer for My name's sake.**"*

Ananias had labeled Paul as hopeless and an enemy of God's, yet the Lord labeled him as a chosen vessel, one who would suffer much for "My name's sake".

What does "name sake" mean? According to Wikipedia, a namesake is when a person, place, or thing is named after another person, place, or thing. Paul was now an adopted child of God, same as every other believer, a name sake.

Have faith in Him. Believe in what He is doing. You are not, and have not been forsaken. You are His name sake. Don't allow ORF to steal this truth from you during the tough times with a lie!

Chapter 13

Not in the bunk house

Looking at our brothers in the Luke 15 story of the prodigal son, we realize that both brothers operated in an orphan spirit which caused them to want an employee/employer relationship with the father.

What did the father do when he saw the prodigal come back to him? Did he do as the son thought and say that he could only be his employee now? That he was only a servant. The father could not deny his own son! The blood that was running through his veins was DNA proof that regardless of what position he took, he was family.

Do you feel that way? Do you feel like a son or a servant? God is not interested in employees. We are to live, breath, and walk as sons. Sons through the blood of Christ and we are now identified through Jesus' DNA flowing in our lives.

God wants us to stop hanging in the bunk house with the servants. He wants us to abide with Him! He wants us to walk in His house, open the fridge and eat! Kill a fatted calf. Make merry with your friends!

Luke 15:11-24 ¹¹ Then He said: "A certain man had two sons. ¹² And the younger of them said to his father, 'Father, give me the portion of goods that falls to me.' So he divided to them his livelihood. ¹³ And not many days after, the younger son gathered all together, journeyed to a far country, and there wasted his possessions with prodigal living. ¹⁴ But when he had spent all, there arose a severe famine in that land, and he began to be in want. **15** Then he went and joined himself to a citizen of that country, and he sent him into his fields to feed swine. **16** And he would gladly have filled his stomach with the pods that the swine ate, and no one gave him anything. **17** "But when he came to himself, he said, 'How many of my father's hired servants have bread enough and to spare, and I perish with hunger! **18** I will arise and go to my father, and will say to him, "Father, I have sinned against heaven and before you, **19** and I am no longer worthy to be called your son. Make me like one of your hired servants."' **20** "And he arose and came to his father. But when he was still a great way off, his father saw him and had compassion, and ran and fell on his neck and kissed him. **21** And the son said to him, 'Father, I have sinned against heaven and in your sight, and am no longer worthy to be called your son.' **22** "But the father said to his servants, '**Bring out the <u>best</u> robe and put it on him, and put a ring on his hand and sandals on his feet. 23 And bring the fatted calf here and kill it, and let us eat and be merry**; **24** for this my son was dead and is alive again; he was lost and is found.' And they began to be merry.

The best robe, the ring, and the sandals, these were things the father used to show all that were at the party that he didn't care the state the son was in, whether he was unwashed, or clean...he was his son! Not an orphan, a son!

The father partied the way our Father parties when His sons come home! God parties and wants us to party too!

In Him we belong...in the Fathers house.

We can never achieve employee of the month in this relationship. There is no way to earn this, and that brings up another facet of this orphan spirit, performance. You can work yourself to the grave trying to be "good" enough for the Father. But the truth is, you already are accepted through Jesus. When we perform, we are only acting.

This employee relationship will never allow us to walk and talk like sons. His love for us is NOT predicated on our performance, good or bad. He sees us through the blood (DNA) of Jesus. He only sees the Son! He cannot love us more and cannot love us less.

Luke 15: 25-32 *25 "Now his older son was in the field. And as he came and drew near to the house, he heard music and dancing. 26 So he called one of the servants and asked what these things meant. 27 And he said to him, 'Your brother has come, and because he has received him safe and sound, your father has killed the fatted calf.' 28 "But he was angry and would not go in. Therefore his father came out and pleaded with him. 29 So he answered and said to his father, 'Lo, these many years I have been serving you; I never transgressed your commandment at any time; and yet you never gave me a young goat that I might make merry with my friends. 30 But as soon as this son of yours came, who has devoured your livelihood with harlots, you killed the fatted calf for him.' 31 "And he said to him, 'Son, you are always with me, and all that I have is yours. 32 It was right that we should make merry and be glad, for your brother was dead and is alive again, and was lost and is found.'"*

When I see the heart of the older brother I am grieved. Sadly, I have seen this in the church, the very <u>body of Christ</u>. I see hearts that are just going through the motions.

It is not our responsibility to be working *for* the Father. He doesn't want that. He wants us working *with* Him. This is not semantics either. If all we are doing is working in the fields, those works are empty and sad. This is especially true because we are not connected to the heart of the Father. If we look at the older brother's heart, it was cold. He didn't care about his own brother; he was only concerned for himself.

Actions speak louder than words, but your attitude speaks much louder than your actions!

We take on this position of servant and do it with a false humility, and it shows. If what we do doesn't line up with the heart of Dad, we have missed it, regardless of our efforts. Sadly we all perform to some degree and usually don't even realize we are. Performance causes us to be defined by our sins, shortfalls and victories.

Performance brings out the acceptance and rejection issues we all deal with. Our society and culture tells us that we are the sum total of our actions, or works, and social circle. Because of those social influences in our lives, it will cause us to look to others for acceptance or identity and not Him.

The truth is that our adoption can only be received, not achieved.

Looking for acceptance is like trying to be adopted. You cannot be adopted unless there is a father that chooses you! How much influence did you have in your physical birth or adoption? How much influence did the sperm and egg that produced you have on the heart of God?

We didn't choose Him, He chose us!

John 15:16 ⁱ⁶ You did not choose Me, but I chose you and appointed you that you should go and bear fruit, and that your fruit should remain, that whatever you ask the Father in My name He may give you.

Zechariah 4:6 'Not by might nor by power, but by My Spirit,' Says the LORD of hosts.

Chapter 14

Self Righteous

Wow!

A lot of my chapters should start with the same word, Wow. God is revealing SO much to me right now that I cannot even begin to explain.

"To teach is to learn twice", Joseph Joubert said.

That is a quote that is really hitting me hard. Do you know the worst part of any argument? The point when you realize you are wrong. It is like pulling a string on your sweater and everything begins to unravel. That describes a lot of my walk with God!

Here I am walking with God, talking with God, in communion with God and, BLAM, here comes an attack. Recently I was being accused of less than honest business practices by a former partner. My integrity is being challenged, by a non believer nonetheless. MY integrity? His is incorrigible, but he is cursing me out and has the gall to set accusations against me!

As I am taking all my thoughts into obedience to Christ, attempting to anyways, I finally realize that I need to reach out to my mentor. I am not winning this battle as much as I feel I need to with my thoughts, because I really want to go reposition this clown's nose to the other side of his face and I <u>know</u> that is wrong. So I reach out to my mentor and confess my sin. He lovingly reminds me of my own messages that I so easily preach to others….ouch.

As I seek God's face, He points out to me some things to consider:

- I am being distracted by this issue and the Lord told me NOT to worry.
- Why am I being so negatively impacted by this?
- Why does what this guy thinks bother me?
- Why can't I get the heart of God regarding this?
- Why am I defending myself? Why do I feel like I need to?

Isaiah 48:10-11 "Behold I have refined you, but not as silver; I have tested you in the furnace of affliction. For My own sake, for My own sake, I will do it; for how should My name be profaned? And I will not give My glory to another."

So here I am allowing you to see my sin, my shortfall, my transparency.

I have been asking my brothers to pray for me for the attack…"I am under attack, (the sky is falling, the sky is falling) I cry out, satan must be mad at my wondrous works" (I joke), but where is the attack really coming from?

Is it really an attack? Or did God allow it to afflict me in order to refine me? Here is what I got.

Why did Jesus NOT defend Himself in the presence of His accusers? The answer is actually so simple that it astounded me when I got it, but then again I am a little slow.

If Jesus defended Himself then it would have been from His own righteousness or "self" righteousness and not from God. God never instructed Him to defend Himself in the presence of His accusers. He was connected to God as a Son and He knew the heart of God.

John 5:19 **19** *Then Jesus answered and said to them, "Most assuredly, I say to you, the Son can do nothing of Himself, but what He sees the Father do; for whatever He does, the Son also does in like manner.*

Jesus didn't need to defend Himself against THIS kingdom. Our Heavenly kingdom is sovereign. Jesus represented that kingdom.

Jesus walked this earth in total victory because He saw and understood God's sovereign rule. He was not affected by satan, nor was there any power in the enemy's camp (the earthly kingdom) due to Jesus' focus on the sovereign Kingdom.

The only power satan has is the power we give him when we come into agreement with him!

Jesus' very Name is Adonai, from the word Hebrew word h113 meaning sovereign.

Isaiah 61:1 NIV **1** *The Spirit of the* **Sovereign** *LORD is on me, because the LORD has anointed me to proclaim good news to the poor. He has sent me to bind up the brokenhearted, to proclaim freedom for the captives and release from darkness for the prisoners*

Sovereignty is government **free** from external control or influence.

Jesus didn't have to answer to this kingdom because the one that He represented trumped this one! His focus was not temporal. His focus was on the eternal.

The Cross was not the end, but the beginning.

That really caused my flesh to burn, because if I defend myself, then I'm focusing on this kingdom....crap. The truth is that God not only told me that I didn't need to defend myself, on the contrary, He said that vengeance was His.

If I am relying on self righteousness it is only because I don't trust in TRUE righteousness. I don't trust that God will defend me as I need to be defended (sounds like revenge). I am not trusting in Him but in myself. Then I realized that this situation is about revealing in me my self-righteousness (remember, attacking MY integrity).

Jesus didn't defend Himself because His hope was in the Father and that Kingdom. He even said that He could call down legions of angels, but He didn't. He was obviously capable of defending Himself as He displayed when He cleansed the temple. Yet He said, I only do what the Father tells me to do and say what the Father tells me to say. He understood His position, His Sonship in the Father, and if I am defending myself then I am obviously NOT. He did this for us!

Then the flesh burning continues, GOD brought this affliction on me to reveal this **about me**....crap again! Whether or not God corrects the issue is NOT the issue. The issue is what am I going to do about what He has revealed about **my** heart?

Will I repent of my sinful ways? Will I accept the discipline and rebuke in order to embrace life, or will I fight Him?

Isaiah 48:9-11 *⁹ "For My name's sake I will defer My anger, And for My praise I will restrain it from you, So that I do not cut you off. ¹⁰ Behold, I have refined you, but not as silver; I have tested you in the furnace of affliction. ¹¹ For My own sake, for My own sake, I will do it; For how should My name be profaned? And I will not give My glory to another.*

God said that it was for His own sake that He would do test us in the furnace of affliction. He would not allow His name to be profaned and would not give His glory to another. He does this because we are called Christians, and that is His name, a part of the Trinity. If we are to go into this world with His name, He will not allow it to be profaned. His glory is only for the family of Christ and he will not give it to another but ALL He has is ours! This is Luke 15 again!

Isaiah 50:6-7 I gave my back to those who struck Me, and my cheeks to those who plucked out My beard; I did not hide My face from shame and spitting. For the Lord God will help Me; therefore I will not be disgraced; therefore I have set My face like a flint, and I know that I will not be ashamed.

If that was Jesus' heart, then as God's representative as a Christian, I need to adopt the same heart.

Jesus knew that because of His relationship with the Father the cross was not the end! IT WAS THE BEGINNING! He knew that the shame being thrown at Him was not the final answer. He said Himself that in three days He would raise from the dead.

He knew what the Father said and that is ALL that matters.

This momentary light affliction is not the end for us. We are born again and we will live with Him for eternity! We need to get this. We need to stop acting like this world means anything, and it is NOT the end for us. So why do we live like it is?

Rick Warren was right; it isn't all about me...need I say, crap again! Sorry if my flavorful language offends.

Chapter 15

We look to man

We look to men for what only God can give. That is why acceptance and rejection is a manifestation that has tripped up many a believer. Most don't recognize that they are even operating in it. They don't realize the lie because it isn't so much about being a son as it is about NOT being orphaned.

Psalm 118:8 ^{8} It is better to trust in the LORD, than to put confidence in man.

Here is an example, using the Luke 15 prodigal son as an example. As a son, we miss the fundamentals of the relationship if we feel that we have to do ANYTHING in order to be accepted and loved by the Father. There are NO strings to this. There is nothing we can do to make Him love us more or love us any less. The cross was unconditional to the very core! We cannot confuse the gifts or jewels in our crowns in heaven with salvation. We cannot connect our performance, or lack thereof here on earth, with unconditional love from Him.

He loves us before we can do anything to earn it. We realize that the acceptance, as well as the rejection we feel, does NOT come from Him. It is not predicated on what we do, think, or feel. This is NOT emotional, this is relational.

Your relationship was created by Him, so stop trying to rationalize it with a finite mind! You are already the accepted, so stop looking to things or people to feel fulfilled with an acceptance that only He can provide. Here is another statement that will be very hard for some to swallow.

Man cannot reject what God has accepted.

If we struggle with rejection by man or circumstances, then we are following man and not God. If we see ourselves through the blood of Jesus as God does, then our vision is corrected to see things from a heavenly perspective.

Jeremiah 29:11 God says He knows the thoughts the thoughts that He thinks towards us. (JVV)

Here is what the Lord said to me regarding that. "Do you? Do you know the thoughts that I think towards you?" Do you know His thoughts? Probably not, because if you did, you would not be tossed to and fro! You would not be distracted and destroyed by this world because you would see it from His perspective. You don't know because you either haven't asked, are afraid to ask, or are not understanding that He wants you to ask! It is His will that you step out in faith and know that He is your safety net, if you are listening and obedient.

We have ears to listen, but we don't hear. We spend so much time trying to tell God what we want rather than to listen to the amazing plan that He has for us!

His plan is WAY better than yours! His plan has eternal gifts, blessings, and rewards. Does yours?

Most Christians who have followed Him for any length of time can testify of at least a half a dozen times that they are thankful God didn't answer a prayer! Think of this, you being mortal and finite, do you give your children everything they ask for? Or do you see it from a more experienced, seasoned position and deny them some of their requests for THEIR benefit. If that is the case, then don't you think that maybe you should trust an infinite, immortal God! Who does everything for your benefit.

Stop looking to man and that includes yourself! Stop trying to be the answer on your own. Don't allow circumstances or situations to define what God is doing. That is a recipe for a true lesson in futility! He has amazing plans for you! He has eternal plans for you! Start looking to him without the mask of an orphan! Ask Him to remove that, so you can fully give Him all the credit.

Sadly enough, many men and women look to other things to satisfy what only God can provide. Sex, booze, porn, groups, clubs, Facebook, etc. They are temporal and will NOT last! They are addictive and progressive and what satisfies today will NOT satisfy tomorrow!

Only God has what will satisfy you now and later!

Your spouse, friends, and even children will all fail you at one point or another. Here is a picture of that. If you went up to a beggar on the street and asked them for $100,000, do you have the right to be angry with them for not giving it to you? No, of course not, because you know that they don't have it to give. Why then do we look to others for what God intends to provide? The orphan spirit is why. We don't trust Him to provide that thing, whatever it is.

A spouse that fails you can cause you to never want to marry again, or even date for that matter. Sometimes we look to a girlfriend or boyfriend to get from them what God intended for us to get from Him. We put a lot of pressure on them to provide something that they can never give us.

A friend can be fickle or even stab you in the back causing you to remove yourself from that relationship. A child is a child, and yet sometimes we put way too much stress on them in order for us to live vicariously through them. I see it all the time in sports. The dad that once was a star, or wanted to be one, will put an amazing burden on his child in order to get the identity and acceptance that should be provided from God.

It is sad to see and yet it happens all the time. We are leaving a trail of scars, and even making orphans of others, by our inability to see that God desires to be our source! We may do this by simply rejecting others before they have a chance to reject us.

I especially see something in the body of Christ that I know the world sees too, competition and strife. What causes us as a body to try to jockey for position? What causes us to step on others to elevate ourselves? It definitely is not from God, and is nothing more than we are looking to be noticed. But to whom are we looking to get noticed? God or man?

The Father has already noticed you, and chose you. He sees you. We don't have to do anything for Him to accept us. I think because of this orphan spirit, that we are looking more to be noticed by other believers, to be considered a "somebody" in the church. To be a part of the "who's who" in the body, or to be envied by other believers that we are a spiritual giant in the body and that God is really into us. His hand is on us! We have got the "bat line" to Heaven...just realized I dated myself with that last reference. ☺

Proverbs talks about this.

Proverbs 25:6-7 ⁶ Do not exalt yourself in the presence of the king, and do not stand in the place of the great; ⁷ For it is better that he say to you, " Come up here," than that you should be put lower in the presence of the prince, whom your eyes have seen.

God is about promotion, but not at the expense of others. Promotion is about God's call and plan.

Identity and acceptance can <u>only</u> come from the Father.

Let go of your dreams to get His. I need to go back to this verse again because it has had such an impact on me.

Proverbs 13:12 ¹² Hope deferred makes the heart sick, but when the desire comes, it is a tree of life.

I struggle a lot with my own dreams and desires, and learning to let go of my dreams to grab a hold of His. It is my own orphan spirit struggle. But that scripture really made me realize I struggle because I don't trust that His plans are really what bring forth life.

If I die to self and allow Him to live through me, then I will have desires placed in my heart that I can trust and believe in, without doubt or fear. I won't miss the call because I will know that it was His plan, and when it is His plan, He is faithful and true to do what He started to do in me. I can take that promise to the bank.

If you have believed in something that you know that you know that you know He has placed in your heart, do not allow anyone or anything take that from you! You have a faithful Father that has a desire FOR you and wants to complete a good work in you. He is Faithful and True, that is His name and is revealed in Revelation:

*Revelation 19:11-13 [11] Now I saw heaven opened, and behold, a white horse. And He who sat on him was called **Faithful and True**, and in righteousness He judges and makes war. [12] His eyes were like a flame of fire, and on His head were many crowns. He had a name written that no one knew except Himself. [13] He was clothed with a robe dipped in blood, and His name is called The Word of God.*

I went a little past my point in that scripture but I just LOVE it. His very name is Faithful and True, and even He cannot deny who He is! That is some good preaching, can I get an AMEN!

Don't look to man, he will only disappoint. Look to God.

Don't look to the church for what God desires to be. **He is your ALL in ALL.** He may use the church to bless but your identity is **in Him**.

Look upward, your future is spectacular! Your blessings are sure and your hope is eternal, that is what it is like…in Dad's house!

Conclusion

The following passage of scripture really sums up what we have been discussing throughout the book. As you are reading it, know that I am declaring it over your life, the reader of this book. You will see a lot of bold font and underlined emphasis on this passage because these truths wage war against the false beliefs that the orphan spirit would rather you not know and understand. God's Word doesn't need or require the extra emphasis, but WE sometimes need it. Read it and make it yours!

*Eph 1:3-14 ³ Blessed be the God and Father of our Lord Jesus Christ, who has **blessed us with every spiritual blessing in the heavenly places in Christ**, ⁴ just as **He chose us <u>in Him</u>** before the foundation of the world, that we should be holy and without blame before Him **in love**, ⁵ having **predestined us to adoption as sons by Jesus Christ to Himself, according to the good pleasure of His will**, ⁶ to the praise of the glory of His grace, by which **He made us accepted in the Beloved**. ⁷ In Him we have redemption through His blood, the forgiveness of sins, according to the riches of His grace ⁸ which He made to abound toward us in all wisdom and prudence, ⁹ having made known to us the mystery of His will, according to His good pleasure which He purposed in Himself, ¹⁰ that in the dispensation of the fullness of the times He might gather together in one all things in Christ, both which are in heaven and which are on earth—in Him. ¹¹ **In Him also we have obtained an inheritance**, being predestined according to the purpose of Him who works all things according to the counsel of His will, ¹² that we who first trusted in Christ should be to the praise of His glory. ¹³ **<u>In Him</u> you also trusted**, after you heard the word of truth, the gospel of your salvation; in whom* *also, having believed, **<u>you were sealed</u> with the Holy Spirit of promise**, ¹⁴ who is the **<u>guarantee of our inheritance</u>** until the redemption of the purchased possession, to the praise of His glory.*

I came across this passage *after* I had finished up the first draft of this book. It spoke to me and kept speaking to me to the point that I felt God really wanted YOU to have it. I also ran across a voice recording that I did on my cell phone while driving one day, and it was just me allowing the Holy Spirit to talk through me. It sums up my thoughts and intents of this book in a way that I wanted to share it with you as well.

From my heart:

The orphan spirit will cause you to latch onto anything and everything else you can latch onto other than God. It is an intentional spirit of rejection. You can be rejected by:

- Church
- Relationship
- Spouse
- Boyfriend/Girlfriend
- Anything that causes you to feel rejected

Because of that feeling of rejection, the orphan spirit causes you to adopt something else to replace that feeling, and replace it with a false (and usually temporary) feeling of acceptance. You will find something or someone that you can "adopt yourself into" to find relief from that emptiness.

Some people will do this with the church. They adopt themselves into a church, diving into all areas of groups and ministries to fill the void, but never really accepting the adoption by the Father into the family of God. They are attached to a church or denomination because of the false sense of acceptance, peace, or whatever it gives them.

That, however, doesn't allow them to walk in the freedom that God intended for them through being a son or daughter.

The only thing that will effectively replace the orphan spirit is a relationship with God, not the body of God, not the ministries, only the actual Godhead himself, the Father.

Those who walk according to the orphan spirit will latch onto all kinds of relationships looking to fill the void. They will find themselves going from relationship to relationship, or thing to thing, but never actually filling the void. Sometimes you see people who are in love with being in love, or sleeping around, which is a false/temporary fix that cannot remain.

Don't look to man for what only God can give.

Don't feel bad about this. Don't feel foolish or frustrated that you have been operating in this. This has been around for all of mankind! ORF hates that we are sons because he never will be one. He is jealous of your relationship with the Father. Jealous of how the Father lovingly, adoringly looks upon YOU. That's what ORF hates. He is deceived, and is a deceiver, because he is actually the orphan. His desire is to create as many "brothers and sisters" in his family as he can. To create his own little family of angry, frustrated, striving, lost, confused, easily irritated, competitive, hopeless siblings.

Our challenge is to not be deceived. The Bible warns us of that.

The only way we can avoid deception is to know the Truth.

Many of us struggle with that simply because believing the deceit is often times easier than believing the Truth.

What is the Truth?

- You are accepted.
- You are chosen
- You are the beloved
- You are sons and daughters
- In Him, you belong
- He has never left you or forsaken you
- He loves you, unconditionally
- You are forgiven
- There are many more promises, look in your Bible! It is God's love letter to you!

Jesus said in *John 14:18 I will not leave you orphans, I will come to you.* That is HIS promise. *Romans 8:14 for as many as are led by the Spirit of God; these are the sons of God.* Every believer is led by the Spirit of God, and because of that, they are adopted into <u>His family</u>.

Adoption does NOT segregate!

Adoption is complete acceptance. It is contractual by God's Word. He is the Judge too. The process of an adoption is a contract that once it has gone before the judge and he has signed off on the paperwork, it is considered to be legal and binding. That part gets me excited, the adoption for us has already been before the Judge and He is also the adoptor! He has already chosen us! It is already legal and binding!

John 15:16 *¹⁶ You did not choose Me, but I chose you and appointed you that you should go and bear fruit, and that your fruit should remain, that whatever you ask the Father in My name He may give you.*

It is not something that you can achieve. It is only something that you can receive. You can only receive it because of the righteousness of Jesus!

Because we are chosen, we can't do anything to make this happen. We can't do anything to make it better or faster or stronger. We *can* deny Him, but that is not the point. If you have accepted Christ, you haven't denied Him, and we are already His kids. The purpose of this book is to point out the areas where we are **not living** like kids, missing out on the fullness that He intended for us to walk in.

I thought if I fasted and prayed that I could get a closer walk, that I could do something that would increase this relationship. I was and am hungry for more of God, but I can't make it happen. Our relationship is not predicated on what I do for Him (fast, pray, works, whatever). It is based solely on what <u>He has already done</u> for me!

You are already noticed, you are already predestined, and you are already chosen.

*Ephesians 1:3-10 ³ Blessed be the God and Father of our Lord Jesus Christ, who has blessed us with every spiritual blessing in the heavenly places in Christ, ⁴ just as **He chose us in Him before the foundation of the world, that we should be holy and without blame before Him in love,** ⁵ <u>**having predestined us to adoption as sons by Jesus Christ to Himself,**</u> **according to the good pleasure of His will,** ⁶ **to the praise of the glory of His grace, by which He made us accepted in the Beloved.** ⁷ In Him we have redemption through His blood, the forgiveness of sins, according to the riches of His grace ⁸ which He made to abound toward us in all wisdom and prudence, ⁹ having made known to us the mystery of His will, according to His good pleasure which He purposed in Himself, ¹⁰ that in the dispensation of the fullness of the times He might gather together in one all things in Christ, both which are in heaven and which are on earth—in Him.*

God has already signed off on the adoption papers for every one of His kids. God knows. That should be enough to explain predestination. But if that isn't enough, try thinking of predestination as pre-adoption into His family.

God knows the ones that will accept Him and the ones that will not. God knew you would! God doesn't want any separation from <u>His kids</u>. That is why He sent Jesus to bring us home.

Now that my point has been made, let's go back to the story in Luke 15, **wasn't there mention of fatted calf....** ☺

For more information about JV Ministries,

Please visit our website:

www.jesusandasixpack.com

Email us at:
info@jesusandasixpack.com

Coming Spring 2012 to paperback and e-book:

Jesus and a 6 pack

Using faith and fitness to not only overcome, but to excel through life's challenges!